Ten Guardian Angels and a Tin Tub

To Jean
Enjoy

Ten Guardian Angels and a Tin Tub

Adalbert Krei

a memoir

Tate Publishing & *Enterprises*

Ten Guardian Angels and a Tin Tub
Copyright © 2011 by Adalbert Krei. All rights reserved.

No part of this publication may be reproduced, stored in a retrieval system or transmitted in any way by any means, electronic, mechanical, photocopy, recording or otherwise without the prior permission of the author except as provided by USA copyright law.

The opinions expressed by the author are not necessarily those of Tate Publishing, LLC.

Published by Tate Publishing & Enterprises, LLC
127 E. Trade Center Terrace | Mustang, Oklahoma 73064 USA
1.888.361.9473 | www.tatepublishing.com

Tate Publishing is committed to excellence in the publishing industry. The company reflects the philosophy established by the founders, based on Psalm 68:11,
"The Lord gave the word and great was the company of those who published it."

Book design copyright © 2011 by Tate Publishing, LLC. All rights reserved.
Cover design by Lauran Levy
Interior design by Christina Hicks

Published in the United States of America

ISBN: 978-1-61739-922-0
1. Biography & Autobiography / Personal Memoirs
2. Biography & Autobiography / Historical
11.01.31

Table of Contents

The New Home	7
Hazardous Games	33
Early Responsibilities	43
Crystal Night: The Beginning of the End	47
War with Russia	69
Cloister Roggenburg	73
The Hell of Phosphorus Bombs	87
Assignment West: Building the Last Defense Line	111
Fifteen-year-old Soldiers: Hitler's Last Reserve	131
Dangerous Desertion	137
Where Are the Rapists and Gangsters?	143
The Heritage of Dangerous Toys	149
The Plunder of an Army Supply Train	155
The Coal Train Adventures	161
The Beginning of Starvation	171
The Black Market	175
Growing Our Own Tobacco	187
Sunday, June 20, 1948: Monetary Reform	191
The Beginning of the Rest of My Life	195
The Last Prank	201
The Start of a New Life for Two	203
Not Again	207
Our Life Is Complete	211
Our Search for Inge's Origin	217

The New Home

The red, paint-flecked truck rolled down the foggy, wet cobblestone road toward its destination, our new home on the outskirts of the city of Remscheid, Germany, located near the city of Cologne.

The precious load consisted of the few belongings our family had accumulated during the difficult times after World War I. The year was 1931. Two and a half years old, I nestled in my mother's lap, which absorbed the impact of the trembling vehicle.

A crashing sound from the rear brought the truck to a sudden stop. My mother carried me with her to the back of the truck. We found that one of the most valuable belongings, our wooden washer, had fallen down and lay broken on the road, one of the steel legs broken off. This was catastrophic for my mother. I remember Mother's often-repeated statement: "There is no excuse for not having clean clothing when you are poor."

My mother, helpless, was looking at the broken washer as my father and my

Mother with my sister Gertrud

seven siblings arrived. My father, out of a job for six years now, had led my brothers and sisters on the ten-mile journey by foot from our former housing, an asylum, to the new residence.

My parents and five of my older siblings. Gertrud, Katie (died early) Mother, Paul, Willi, and John

With the help of my oldest brother, John, who was eighteen years old, the washer went back on the truck. After a half-mile, we reached the end of our journey.

The home we were about to move into was huge from my perspective. It used to be the local school, converted into residential housing for large families. The building housed eight family units with a total of fifty-eight children.

When we came into our new home, it was so different from the one we just left behind. There were wooden floors, not stone. The three rooms had high ceilings. The room that would be our kitchen, dining, and living room included a faucet and a sink with running cold water. The other two rooms, one of them large, were our bedrooms. The smaller one with the large window facing the street was large enough to place two beds inside. The seaweed-filled mattresses were firm but comfortable. One bed was for my parents and the other for the four of us younger children. Two had to sleep at the head of the bed and the other two at the foot.

The outhouse was located at the edge of the forest, opposite our apartment. To get to it we had to go all the way around the house. It was a rather large building with eight separate stalls, one for each family. Since it was a relatively long walk to the outhouse, we supplemented a bucket for the night, placed in one corner of the small hallway. Every morning someone had the duty to carry the bucket to the outhouse to empty.

It is sometimes amazing how little things often stay in our mind. When we moved into our new home and I took a first look at the large, empty rooms, I found a little tin motorcycle toy with a winding key attached to it. Maybe the former resident left it there, and this made me very happy. Strangely, I had only that day to play with the toy motorcycle; then it was gone. I liked this toy so much that I still searched for it years later but never found it again.

Only very small bits of memories of our previous home stayed with me. There was one memory I did not forget, and that was the cold, stone floor. The wooden floor at the new home felt warm and comfy compared to our old place. I especially liked the atmosphere outside of our new home, the surrounding forests interrupted only by the green meadows. With so many playmates at our new home, this was a perfect playground for us. While I was too little, all my older siblings had chores to perform, and this gave me more time to play. At night, we all looked forward to taking our place in our beds. Two on the head of the bed and two at the foot. Then our storytelling would begin, when I was about three or four years old. Every night we took turns to make up a story until everybody was fast asleep.

My favorite story I made up was about my dream vehicle, which consisted of a tin tub that served as our bathtub. Every Saturday, Mother boiled a few kettles of water on our large, coal-heated stove. She could only boil enough water for one filling of the two feet large tin tub, and that had to do for the four youngest of us.

Naturally, the tub was much larger in the stories I amused my sisters with. I was behind the steering wheel, and in my fantasy, it would take me any place I wanted it to go. I could drive through the forest, and my tin tub was able to drive up large trees. It even could fly through the air to distant stars and to the moon. I felt that nothing could stop me. Of course, all my sisters accompanied me in my phantasm.

There was plenty of food in my tin tub. I would ask one of my sisters to bring me a French roll with liver sausage, which was always in my mind since I tasted it once at my sister's communion. From all the food in my tin tub, every one of my sisters had a choice. The most in demand was cake and cookies.

My sisters Maria, Anita and Franzi

There were times when I asked my mother for a sandwich because I was hungry, and she answered, "Lick salt and you will be thirsty too." She just did not have the means to put enough food on the table. The suffering of having not enough food during my father's unemployment had a profound impact on my mother. She was a great cook, and from only one bone she could make a good-tasting soup that lasted for three days. At night she often served milk soup. How she kept the little food we had without spoiling for a few days without ice is still a mystery to me.

When fall harvest arrived and the cabbage and beans were inexpensive, I was ordered to go to a local store to pick up a cabbage shredder. The rent for one day was fifty cents. The whole family was occupied grating the cabbage and filling the large stone pots, turning, during the winter, into sauerkraut. Another large stone pot was filled with cut beans, and the stone pots were then transported into the basement.

My mother was very religious, and she found her strength through the church and through her prayers. I observed that every time before she cut the first slice from a loaf of bread, she held the bread on her chest and with the large knife made a motion of a cross on the underside of the bread. "Give us this day our daily bread," she prayed. She explained to me that she was blessing the bread, and she repeated this ceremony until she died at the age of eighty.

Soon after our settlement, I met some new friends. There was so much for us to do, and we were able to enjoy our childhood to the fullest.

Surrounding the house was a large forest with tall trees. Down in the valley was a wide river. The large field behind the house was a perfect soccer field. Rolling some old rags into a ball had to do as a soccer ball. It was even more fun when some of the older kids participated. Since I was chosen as the goalkeeper and missed a few balls, I lost on popularity.

The forest was ideal to build our treasure chest. We dug a hole into the ground and deposited our treasure, anything from pieces of colored glass to the little wooden boats we had carved from tree bark, and covered the hole with a piece of tarpaper or whatever we found that suited as a cover. The hiding place was then covered with earth and camouflaged. The secret place was so well hidden that sometimes I never found it again, or maybe it fell victim to one of my friends' robbery. The treasure chest was a place where we could hide things that seemed valuable to us. We dreamed that those treasures would someday turn into real treasures.

With so many children at our new home, there was always somebody that came up with a new idea. Yes, there was my cousin Siegfried, who lived in a house next door, who was spoiled with toys we never dreamed of. I was always happy when he invited me to play with him. Even though he had all his bought toys, he was thrilled to play with our self-built ones. The only toys I remember receiving were at Christmas, but most of those were built by my older brothers and sisters. The one I remember well was the puppet-show set all for me. It consisted of a box with a front opening. Some leftover wallpaper decorated the outside. My older brothers and sisters created the puppets from plaster and newspaper. They worked on them late into the nights before Christmas to finish the puppets on time.

In springtime, after a hard rainfall when the water gushed out of the quells at the forest ground, we built a dam to hold the water. With our little carved ships, we dreamed that we were crossing the big ocean to a land far away to visit the brave Indians. When the forest ground was dry, we went to the river down in the valley and set the ships into the rushing water and ran along the shore until our ships floated away and finally disappeared.

Although we all played together, each of us had some close friends, and Alfred was one of my closest. When I was about six years old and Alfred was a year younger, we were inseparable. At times, Kathryn and Elisabeth, who both were at our age, accompanied us on our excursions through the forest and down to the valley. On one of those outings, curiosity set in when the girls were watching when Alfred and I were able to stand up peeing against a tree. I don't remember who made the proposition to check each other out, but we all agreed to investigate the difference between boys and girls. The phrase "playing doctor" came from taking our clothing off. We promised one another we wouldn't tell anyone. After this happened, I knew that it was wrong because my conscience told me so. Kathryn told her mother about the games we played.

From Left: My friends Alfred, Elizabeth, and Katie

On that day, I had the duty to help my older sister, Gertrud, carry the dirty laundry from our apartment to the joint laundry room, located at the opposite side of the house. While we were carrying our heavy load around the outside of the building, Kathryn's mother, who was at the third-floor window, was screaming to my sister the bad things we had done. As soon as we got to the laundry room where Mother was waiting, Gertrud could not wait to tell her how bad her son was.

Whatever happened next I remember vaguely. I woke up on a pile of dirty laundry. My face was full of dried blood, and through the thick fog of the room, I noticed my mother pushing the three-foot handle of her washer with a monotone motion, back and forth. The thick fog, caused by the boiling laundry in the large kettle, made me glad that I could not see her face because I was so ashamed.

That night, as so often before, I had to go to bed early without food. This was the most severe punishment my siblings and I could receive. My siblings and I respected my oldest brother, John, almost more than our parents. He was even stricter than our father and mother. He taught us to eat right and sit properly at the table. John disciplined us and taught us respect, honesty, and morals, but I did not always follow his teachings. My father was very lenient with us children. I think that he had some guilty feelings for not having a job for so long. John recognized this and, as the oldest of my siblings, thought that he needed to take on the responsibility of my father.

Since we did not possess any toys to play with, we made our own. One of our favorite activities was striking a wheel or a circle with a short stick and running next to the wheel. We would keep on striking it to keep it rolling. My lucky day came when I found a car tire at a dump, which made me the happiest kid around.

Nobody would top this one. Since there were not that many cars around, a tire was not often to be found. I had the perfect hiding place under the stairs in the hallway outside our apartment.

Two of my sisters had to clean the hallway on weekends. While I was busy playing outside, John appeared at the window and told me to move the tire to the basement. When I dared to refuse, because I was too busy playing with my friends, he said, "All right, then we will cut the tire and make soles for our shoes from it," and closed the window. Believing that he was just kidding, I hesitated at first, but then I changed my mind and ran to my hiding place. As I arrived, I found my favored toy already sliced in half. That was one of the biggest hurts, and I would have given anything if it could have been undone.

John was the one that suffered most when we were children. He realized the grief of my parents. Also not being able to get a job to help, he took his destiny in his own hands. He wanted to not depend on my parents and give them one less mouth to feed. He was a master in his field as a carpenter and even built his own guitar.

John left home and walked with two of his best friends throughout Germany. After they made it over the mountain range of the Alps, they arrived one and a half years later at the city of Rome, working on their journey for farmers or playing their guitars. This earned them the necessities to go on. When John left, I felt that I lost the protection of my older brother. On the other hand, I was glad I was not being constantly reprimanded by him for a while, and I think that some of my siblings thought the same, while my parents missed his support.

When John finally came back home, I remember him unpacking some juicy oranges from his backpack for us children. So much had happened during the time of his absence. Since 1933, Germany had a new government led by Adolf Hitler, who called himself the Fuehrer, meaning "the leader." He promised to lead Germany out of the worst depression the world had ever seen, caused by the Treaty of Versailles. At first, it seemed that he kept his pledge. Slowly the economy improved, and a new program was started, the Winterhilfswerk, meaning "Winter Relief Organization." This relief effort was organized by the Nazi establishment and was designed to provide food, clothing, coal, and other items to less fortunate Germans during the inclement months. This was, of course, an immense help for us. To finance this large relief endeavor, members of the Nazi party and of the Hitler Youth collected, with their red can, from anyone but concentrated especially on the small businesses. If anyone refused to contribute, he was labeled as a miser. This happened to our grocer, who had a small store located in his house. The next day there were signs throughout the area with the word *miser*, his name, and his address.

I think that Hitler received most support from the German people for the repudiation of the Treaty of Versailles. The French had to leave the occupation of the Rhineland, and there was no more free delivery of coal and machinery to France as imposed by the Treaty of Versailles.

In July 1935, we had an addition to our family. My sister Heidi was born, and now there were nine living children. Two of my sisters died previously. Shortly after my sister's birth, my mother's health started deteriorating. The constant worrying about her family, as well as necessary gall bladder surgery, gnawed at her health, and our church sent her for six weeks to a recuperation home.

My father, with the help of a sister of our church, had to take care of the rest of us. During my mother's absence, he acquired a job at a small factory. I was six years old and remember that day. As my father carried Heidi in his arms, we walked to the tram station for the arrival of my mother. On our way to the station, I had to promise I would not talk to Mother about Father's job, which he started shortly before Mother came home. After our happy reunion with my mother, my father could no longer wait. I never saw two people happier when he told my mother the good news of his employment.

In April of that year, I had my first day of school. I have to admit that I had a feeling of envy when I watched the arrogant, rich kids carrying their large, cone-shaped school bags. It was custom for anyone that could afford it to have the three-foot cone with candies and chocolate. I was a little resentful, since we were unable to afford any those things. The first day of school was short. I remember that our teacher told us a nice story about a little boy who was supposed to have his first day of school but instead ended up sleeping in a stork's nest he found on the roof of a house on his way to school. After the story, we learned to write the first letter of the alphabet.

We were Catholic, and the next Catholic school was about six miles from home. The long walk every day, with my siblings and friends, was both strenuous and fun. Twice a week we had to attend church service before school. That meant leaving home two hours before school started.

I made more friends at the school, good and bad ones. The twins, Karl and Hans, were also from a poor family. During our break, while all the teachers walked back and forth on our school playground keeping an eye on the playing children, Hans would sneak back into our classroom and steal two marks out of the teacher's purse. He did this more than once.

We condemned his action, but when he came back from the store across the street with cigarettes, we snuck behind the outhouses at the corner of the schoolyard and joined in and smoked. It was, of course, not smoking in the usual sense. We were just eight-year-olds trying to imitate the grown-ups. We just took a few puffs and then discarded the cigarettes. If we were caught, we would be punished with some strikes on our rear with that familiar stick.

Then came a day our teacher called our names—Karl, Hans, and I—to stay after school. At first, we did not know the reason and feared the worst. Why just us and not the others that also were involved? The surprise came after the last of the students left the classroom.

The teacher asked us to come to the front and pointed under her desk. There stood a big basket full of delicious pears. Our teacher ordered us to share these with each other and then with our siblings. We responded with joy. She had chosen us because she knew that the exquisite fruit was not on our food plan and she did not want to shame us in the presence of the other students.

Hans was a clown sometimes and not fearful. We had this very eccentric teacher with a beard, and his rimless glasses sat on the tip of his nose; his name was Monshausen. He was our sports and music teacher. During one of our gymnastics classes, the teacher caught Hans smoking a cigarette. He received the usual punishment. While he touched the tip of his toes, he received two strikes with what our teacher called "have mercy," the thin, half-inch, flexible stick that made a whistling sound when it flew through the air on its way to the victim's behind. Most of us were very familiar with the excruciating pain. Hans swore he would pay the teacher back for the humiliation, and he picked the next music class to get his revenge.

Monshausen's favored instrument was his violin, which he operated like a master. Before class started, Hans snuck into the classroom to hide inside the large closet, containing the many rolls of maps used in our geography classes.

As soon as Monshausen started his artistic demonstration with his violin, Hans, in the closet, tried to mimic the sound of the violin. Monshausen was full of anger and searched for the source of the interruption. After a few of those intriguing noises, he was furious at not finding the source. Suddenly, he ran over to the closet, opened the doors, and lost all control. With a loud crash, the glorious violin landed on Hans's head, leaving the broken violin dangling on its strings from the handle.

I hated school, particularly homework. It took away from my playtime. When I hurried to get my homework done and it was not to the satisfaction of my mother, she spit on my slate plate, wiped everything off with her apron, and said, "Start over."

After a few of those times, I knew better. I did my homework on the way home on one of those tin garbage cans that were standing in front of every house. Then when I came home, I stated, "I don't have any homework." The result was bad grades. This behavior of mine lasted only a short time until my mother found out and consequently watched my homework from then on.

There was one girl in my class I liked a lot, and it seemed that she liked me. She was a child of a wealthy family. Her parents owned a medium-sized company. Usually she went to and from school by streetcar, which we, of course, could not afford. Sometimes she walked with me the long way home.

On one of those days, when we got to her house, a villa, she invited me to come in with her. After she told her mother who I was, she wanted to show me her room. I could not believe that somebody could have his or her own room. I was astounded by the large jar full of candies standing on the cupboard. She offered some to me before I went home. After that, she never walked home with me again.

When her mother found out I lived at the "old school," our home, she did not allow her daughter to play with me. The only reputation we had was that we were poor.

The year was 1936. John left home again and went to the city of Munich. He found a job as a carpenter to work on Hitler's personal house, named the "brown house." He had to work on the staircase.

When Hitler stopped by to inspect the remodeling of the house one day, all the workers had to stop working. John refused. He distrusted Hitler's politics, openly showed his dislike, and kept on working. John was fired. Shortly after this incident, he returned home and found a job at a furniture company. Not long after, he and his friends joined the Catholic underground movement against the Nazis. Their name: "The Travelers of the Cross."

My parents were not in agreement about John's decision. While my mother was completely in union with John, my father was more worried about his security and tried to change his mind. I paid no attention at that time. I was just too young to realize the dangerous step John made.

My friends and I played our own risky games when we found a millstone leaning against the wall of the deserted factory. With joint forces and great endeavor, we achieved in getting the monster stone that was bigger than us into motion. Once we reached the edge of the steep hill, gravity took over. Slowly at first but then faster and faster, we sent him on his journey down to the valley. On his way, he snapped small trees like matchsticks and crossed a road until deep down in the valley it came to rest. Only then we realized how irresponsible our action was and were happy that no one was injured.

One person that was always watching us play was Menne. He was about thirty years old and retarded. His job was to tend a flock of goats. Good in nature, he was a great playmate for us children. The only atrocious characteristic was the foam on his mouth when he talked. We all liked him in spite of the big age difference; he played as if he was one of us. The only time I saw him get mad—the foam on his mouth was even more visible—was when we tried milking his goats. He also introduced us to an herb by the name of sorrel, a leaf-like plant with a sour, juicy taste that grew in abundance all around us. We picked and stacked many leaves until we had a package about one to two inches thick. Then, with our mouths watering and great anticipation, we took a large bite. Most likely it was the perfect substitute for the missing vitamins during that time.

One day, Menne and his goats did not show up anymore. They told us he had to go to a hospital. In later years, we learned that he had joined the many other insane people that did not fit into the frame of the Nazi intellectuality of a clean and healthy super race.

Fall was always exciting because it was kite-flying time. At a local carpentry factory, we asked for two or three thin wooden strips, depending on the shape of the kite we wanted to build. For the needed paper, we begged for some packaging paper from another small company across the street.

By that time the apples at the adjacent orchard were ready to be harvested. It was to our advantage when one of our kites got caught in one of the apple trees. With the permission of the orchard owner to retrieve our damaged kite, we never missed the chance to fill our pockets with some of the juicy apples.

Sometimes we took a shortcut to the orchard where all those delicious apples were just waiting to be harvested. The way was over a piercing iron fence. One day Bubbes, one of my friends, and I decided to try the shortcut. He climbed over the fence first; my turn was next. For some reason, I slipped, and one of those pointed spears entered right into my lower jaw and chin. I was hanging there helpless. I struggled like a goat on a meat hook, but with the help of Bubbes, I got free again.

After our local first aid man cleaned and bandaged the wound, I was okay. I do not know if it was the memory of my first experience, but when we tried again I slipped again, and this time I was hanging on the spike with my right lower arm, just missing my main artery.

From then on, I had too much respect for the fence to try ever again.

Werner, another friend, was a real artist at making kites. I still do not know how he made his ideas fly. He could make them to reach the highest elevation, and they remained up there all afternoon. We sent letters up to the kite by puncturing a hole into piece of paper, leading the string through the hole, and the wind did the rest.

Werner also already had a job at a laundry company delivering laundry. He had his little four-wheel cart with a shaft to pull and steer the cart. When he asked me at some point to come along, I did. After we loaded the laundry onto his wagon, we pulled the cart until we arrived at a point where the road was going down the hill. Werner told me to sit on the top of the cleaned laundry. He himself made some room up front to sit. Then he put his legs around the pulling shaft, and there we went down the steep hill. The cart picked up speed very fast. Then suddenly, on a slight curve, Werner lost control. The cart made a swift turn to the right and then tipped over, burying both of us with the once-so-tidy packaged load of laundry. Amazingly, neither of us was hurt, but it was the end of Werner's job.

Not long after this juncture, Werner died of scarlet fever. We were very sad to lose him as a friend, but mostly we lost our greatest kite builder.

This dreadful disease captured so many others. My sister Heidi, the baby of our family, was now two years old. She also contracted the disease. My parents had to admit her to the hospital. Everyone in our family feared for her. When we went to visit her, we only could see her from an outside window while a nurse was holding her. My thoughts went back to the times when I sometimes handled her so roughly when she was just a few months old.

Often I had to take care of her. My mother placed her into a stroller, and I took her for a ride. As soon as my mother was out of sight, I used the stroller as an imaginary racing car. I went with her through any obstacle I could find. Sometimes I lost control, and the baby carriage turned over. I put Heidi right back into it and started all over.

When I saw her through the hospital window, I felt so sorry for what I did. When she finally came home, looking almost like a skeleton, I promised that from now on I would be better and would take care of her. I kept my promise.

My brother Willi, twenty-one years old then, was ordered into the German National Labor Service, a pre-military organization wherein every young man had to serve for two years before he was enlisted into the German army. The purpose of this organization was to convert wasteland into the so much needed farmland, build roads, and go through pre-military training.

John, for some reason, was lucky. He never had to enlist into the labor service and worked at the carpenter workshop. He went back to night school and graduated with his master's degree in carpentry.

Paul, my youngest brother, then sixteen years old, turned out to be a top gymnast. He almost made it to the 1936 Olympics but was not old enough. Paul and I never would have had the opportunity to train as gymnasts if it were not for Hitler's obsession with a healthy and sporty German youth. It was highly promoted. Almost all sport activities were free of charge. Paul also started his apprenticeship as a tool and die maker when he was fourteen years old.

During my school years, he was always high on a pedestal. The phrase, "If you want to be like your brother Paul, you have a long way to go," still rings in my ears. He was a straight-A student throughout his school years and continued his top achievements during his apprenticeship. I wanted so much to be like my brother, but the steady emphasis that was put on my brother's achievements turned me off, and I grew stubborn.

When I was eight years old, Paul took me to his gymnastic club. With his guidance and coaching, I too turned into a first-class gymnast. Thanks to him, I earned many first places.

When I was ten years old, Paul introduced me to the magic of photography. Our small room we called the "caboose," off from our main room, was dark and had no window. Here he kept his chemicals for film developing. I remember the day he took a picture of me, dipped the glass plate into the chemicals, and like magic, slowly my picture appeared on the glass plate. This was fascinating to me. From that day on, photography never left me.

My fascination with photography drove me to the craziest ideas. When I found my brother Willi's camera in his drawer and noticed it was loaded with film, I decided to walk with my friend Heinz to the bridge of Müngsten. The bridge, spanning over a deep valley, is the highest rail bridge in Europe. It was about seven miles from home and connected the city of Solingen with my hometown, Remscheid.

Heinz and I decided to climb through the construction from one side of the valley to the other. When we

Bridge at Müngsten

almost reached the top of the bridge, about 360 feet off the ground, I had the idea to create some pictures with Willi's camera no one had ever created. I asked Heinz to brace himself and to hold my legs. Then I climbed over an I-beam and let myself slowly head first down.

Dangling in the air and just depending on Heinz to hold on to my legs, I snapped some unusual shots from under the bridge. When we came down on the other side of the bridge, some workers accosted us. They gave us quite a lecture about our dangerous game but let us finally go. I left the film in the camera and placed the camera back in Willi's drawer. Willi always wondered what those pictures were of when he had the film developed, and he found out the truth many years later.

With some other duties, I had to take over the job of getting groceries at the local store. Usually the store was full of women talking about all the news in the neighborhood. Sometimes it seemed like hours for my turn just to get some flour or sugar.

Mr. Freidhof was thin in stature, and his wife was exactly the opposite. I always watched with great amusement the way the two passed each other at the small aisle behind the counter. Sometimes I imagined what would have happened if he would have been as round as his wife was.

While I was waiting for my turn, I killed the time by searching through the large barrel of chicken feed, which was standing next to the herring and pickle barrels. Once in a while I was lucky and found some of those little dried fish. When the grocer was in a good mood, he reached into a special large can where he kept the broken candies and offered one to me. That was worth all the waiting.

Other times I was sent to the local butcher to get a hundred grams, approximately a quarter pound, of bratwurst for my mother's vegetable dinner. Standing at the counter, I kept a very close eye on the scale and how close the woman would hit the hundred grams. Often she had to add a small slice to it to make it just right. Maybe she added a little piece because she knew what would happen to it. On the way home, it was a delight to feel the slice of sausage melting in my mouth. If the slice turned out to be a little thick and that one was gone, Mother was angry with the butcher, who, as she said, could not be trusted. She had no suspicion that I could have eaten the missing piece. Then again, did she know and just want to fill my conscience with guilt?

On one occasion, I was sent by my mother to the grocer for potatoes. I was alone in the store, and the woman had to go outside to get the potatoes. For a while, I was eyeing the chocolate bars in the glass enclosure. Suddenly I could not resist and let one of the bars disappear into my pants pocket. At her return, the woman seemed not to notice the missing bar. On my way home, my conscience began to agitate me, and I thought about my mother's words: *God sees everything you do.* With this in my mind, I crawled into the densest shrubbery I could find. While I was telling myself, *There is no way that the Lord is able to see me here,* I enjoyed the rare delicacy. For years, when I entered the store, I had to face the woman's staring look of indictment. This was punishment enough.

One day an older woman walked down the street and interrupted our play. She was well known in our neighborhood and lived in a small villa. The woman was the widow of a once wealthy factory owner. Her apparel seemed like it was from the Victorian time, and her black dress reached all the way to her ankles. On this day, as so many times before, she wore a large black hat and disdainfully passed our house. We had a field day when we noticed that the dress she was wearing was in the back tucked into her white, lacy, embroidered underpants. She never would lower herself to talk to any of us. Now this day was our day. We surrounded her, and we were laughing and making fun of her, but she had no idea that the commotion was all about her dress tucked into her underpants. She turned around and walked as speedily as she was able toward her home, her dress still tucked in her underpants.

Hazardous Games

Danger often accompanied our playtime. At times, I went with Andrew, the brother of Kathryn, to their basement. We found under all the other treasures a box with eight large shotgun cartridges. In addition, we found a bag full of aluminum coins from the time of the big inflation in the 1920s. They were, of course, out of circulation. After I asked Andrew for some coins, he gave me a few. Then we decided to take the projectiles and have ourselves a blast. We went to our soccer field, where a mound of large cobblestones was piled up. We took one of the stones, set it on the ground, and laid the eight cartridges on the surface. With extensive effort, I lifted one of the cobblestones above my head to smash the cartridges. Suddenly someone grabbed the stone away from me. I felt the spanking hand of one of our neighbors. He probably saved me from having my body saturated with pellets or worse.

Andrew was about two years older than I was. Since he was already an altar boy, he was going to teach me the trick of the trade. In his bedroom, we cleaned up his dressing table. We folded a newspaper in half and cut a hole in the seam of the paper, and this served as the priest's vestments. The chalice we made from aluminum foil we found in empty cigarette packages.

It was a very sacred moment when Andrew was playing the priest and I was kneeling on the floor during our make-believe Mass. I was only waiting for the communion in the form of a cookie that Andrew's mother volunteered and also some raspberry juice that we used as the wine for the church service.

It was the time when the yearly fair with all the rides and the usual things a fair has to offer came to town. To earn some free tickets for a merry-go-round, some school friends and I offered our services to help with the erection of the fun promising carousels. It was not too often that one of us was accepted. However, if we were, we worked all afternoon. After we completed the work, we were told to come back another day to pick up our free tickets. Of course, when we came back, they had some excuse and did not give us the promised free ride we worked so hard for.

Standing on the outside of the merry-go-round, I found an opening on one side. I crawled through the opening beneath the construction and looked for some coins that might have been lost from the riders. Sometimes I was lucky. On one of those occasions, the owner spotted me crawling around on the ground between the frames, dangerously close to the turning spider of the carousel, which could crush me. Not realizing the danger and engaged with my treasure hunt, I noticed the man came toward me. I felt a sudden pain at my rear end caused by the owner's foot. Panicky, I fled the scene.

Once outside, I was now determined to risk everything as I felt some of the old worthless coins from my friend's basement in my pocket. Now I had the guts to put some of them into circulation. Up to now, I had been too scared to use them at the fair; even so, the coins at that time looked so much like the coins that were in circulation. When I passed by a lottery booth and the person that was selling the ticket accepted one of my false coins without suspicion, I got braver. Surprised that my number on my unlawfully purchased ticket showed me as a winner, I walked up to the booth and traded my ticket for a three-inch globe mounted on a little stand. I was happy about the globe, but with a guilty feeling, I started the long way home.

I must have walked about half of the way when my guilt turned into panic. I could not take this beautiful globe home without being questioned by my mother. Turning around and walking that long way back with the intention of returning the dishonestly acquired property, I tried to tell myself that I did not like it anyway and returning it was the right thing to do.

When I returned to the place of my crime, I thought first I should just place the globe back with the others. Then I noticed those large chocolate bars, and I asked if I could exchange the globe for one of those. When they accepted my trade, I took the chocolate to give to my mother. For some reason, that calmed my bad conscience because I would make Mother happy through my wrongdoing. When I was on my way home again, there was the temptation to have just a little piece of that chocolate. I assured myself that Mother would be happy with three-quarters of the chocolate bar. When I got home, I told Mother that I received the chocolate for helping set up the carousel. I wouldn't dare tell her that I paid for the lottery ticket with false coins. Mother divided the chocolate between my sisters.

We all were highly skilled to build a bow and make the most effective arrows to go with it. We knew exactly from what tree to cut the materials that we needed for the bows and arrows to shoot at each other. The skill to pick the right branches was handed down from the older children. The one that was the most skilled in shooting at a target was Bubbes. On one occasion, he was shooting at me. Thinking back, I think it was more coincidental and not the skill that landed one of his arrows through my mouth and into my throat. Not being able to scream, I ran home. My mother was furious while she was pulling the arrow out of my throat. The disablement of speaking and the painful intake of food were punishment enough. It was not until I reached adulthood that I realized how much anxiety I must have caused my mother.

Twice a week the milkman came down the bumpy road. His horse, called Emma, pulled the heavy load of milk cans. All the kids immediately surrounded the horse. The old man knew how much we admired his horse. He invited those of us who wanted to see the little pony he said was in his stable at home. He was obviously very lonely on his journey between the widely spread houses. He usually picked two of us to climb onto the seat and accompany him. He said that at the end of the ride he would show us the pony and promised that we could take that pony back home if we wanted. Of course, when we reached his home after the long ride, there was no pony. He told us that the pony probably ran away. So we started, terribly disappointed, the long way home on foot.

In the wintertime, when the snow was high, the milkman delivered the milk with his large sled. It was a lot of fun when some of the kids who were fortunate enough to possess a toboggan tied it behind the milkman's sled and let the horse pull them for a while.

For those of us that had no sled, we entertained ourselves by making skid paths from ice. On one of those occasions, we had a skid path close to an outside staircase of about eight steps. I had the splendid idea of using the stairs like a ski jump. I took an extra long start, ran as fast as I could, skidded with high speed on the ice, and sailed high through the air down the stairs. When I landed on my hands, I felt a terrible pain in my left lower arm. When I looked down, I started to scream. My arm did not look the same anymore. My wrist was totally out of shape. It was as if the bones were ready to bulge out of my skin and doubled up. My only thought was, *Is this the end of my life?*

Screaming, I ran home where my older sister Franzi looked at my arm. While she grabbed a ruler to use it as a splint, I asked her, "Do I have to die now?" On our forty-five-minute walk to the hospital, I must have asked that question many times. When we finally arrived, they took me into surgery and put me under anesthetic. When I woke up, I felt nauseated and stared at the big cast on my arm. After wearing the cast for six weeks, I had to go back to the hospital to have the cast removed. By then, it was early spring.

The next day we played in the meadow close to our house. While I was teasing some other kids until they were crying, my brother Paul was also present. He told me numerous times to stop the teasing, but I did not listen. He got up from the grass and started to come after me to stop me. Since I was very nimble, he had a hard time capturing me. Finally he reached out to grab my back but instead gave me a push, and I landed on my left shoulder. I felt a sharp pain. I knew something was wrong.

This time my mother took me to the hospital. When we arrived and the doctor examined me, a nurse asked me, "Aren't you the boy we just yesterday took the cast off your arm?" I said, "Yes!" The doctor found out that I had a broken collarbone. After they were finished with the bandage, the nurse left the room and returned shortly after with the biggest chocolate bar I had ever seen. While she gave me the chocolate, she also gave me the advice to never come back again.

Bordering the orchard was an old, abandoned factory building that had hundreds of tiny windows. One day we had the idea to bet which one of us could smash the most windows. Armed with plenty of rocks, we took position. As we started to throw the rocks, we noticed the woman who was the caretaker of the property come running down the path toward us. As soon as we saw her coming, we started running but went right into a dead corner, surrounded by a thick hedge.

Since there were five of us, it took longer than we had anticipated to crawl through the small opening in the hedge. By the time it was my turn, I was the last one to make it through the hole; it was too late. Our pants at that time had a flap in the back that could be unbuttoned when we had to go to the bathroom. Just when I was halfway through the hedge, I felt somebody grab a hold of that flap. I struggled for my life. My friends realized my situation and tried to pull me through the hole. It seemed the hand on my pants was stronger. Then, with a pop, all the buttons of my flap came loose, and my naked behind was at the mercy of the pursuer. Underpants were a luxury we could not afford. While she was beating my behind like drummer's beat, my buddies still tried to free me, and after what seemed like an eternity, they finally were successful.

When I came home, still holding my broken flap up not to show my mistreated red body part, my mother was readily informed about our prank. Therefore, the flap came down again, and my mother expressed her dislike of our doings on the surface of my body, which was still burning from the pain of my earlier treatment. She took my pants off to replace the lost buttons. I went crying into the dark room we called the caboose. In there was the old closet where we just kept old rags. As so many times before, it was my sanctuary where I would sit on the rags, close the doors, and remain until the pain was gone.

Occasionally my mother would search through those rags to find something that was useful to make clothing for us. I remember the time she found an old coat. Since I didn't have a coat, she separated an old one, turned the inside out, and sewed, with the help of some women from our church, a new coat for me. I was so proud when I went to church wearing my coat for the first time. It was early spring, and it was a cool day. The pockets were soft and warm, and I loved that coat.

The same day in the afternoon, I found this little pocket-sized diary in my brother Paul's drawer. Since I was curious what was in there, I put it into my pocket and went outside. I asked my friend Alfred to come with me to the field, our playground. The grass at that time was tall and dry. We lay in the grass and studied my brother's little booklet. To our disappointment, nothing in the book was of any interest to us. Being afraid to take the book back home, we made the decision to burn the book.

Alfred had some matches, and with his help, the book started burning. What we did not take into consideration was that the wind was blowing quite hard. Before we could do anything, the tall dry grass caught fire, and in no time, a burning inferno surrounded us. The only resource we had to extinguish the fire was our clothing. I took my "new" coat with those soft, warm pockets and tried to extinguish the flames. It was a losing battle.

By now many neighbors arrived to the rescue. When the fire was finally out, I realized that I left my coat somewhere on the ground. A terrible thought came into my mind while I was searching through the now blackened grass. My fear turned into reality when I finally found just a small narrow strip with some buttonholes. My beautiful coat was history.

I do not know why I took the remnant home with me, hiding it under the stairway in our hallway. During the next few days, my mother was in despair and presumed that somebody stole my coat. This lasted only until the next weekend, when her despair turned into anger. That was when one of my sisters, who was cleaning under the stairway, came into the room swinging the burned piece like a scalp. My mother only made the statement that from now on I just had to do without a coat.

Early Responsibilities

Shortly after I turned nine years old, I got my first paper route for the church newspaper. Every week I had to walk many miles for the delivery. The parishioners were spread over a large area, and the delivery lasted mostly until late at night.

At times when I was lucky, I received a few pennies or a cookie for my service. With my pennies, I would go to a nearby bakery and ask for five pennies' worth of pretzel crumbs. When I arrived at home, I asked my mother for some milk. Then I mixed the crumbs with the milk. This treat was worth all those miles and the agony of that day.

Having a paper route was not the only job I had. After my brother John built a rabbit stall, I was responsible for ten to fifteen rabbits. Every afternoon I collected from the surrounding field a large burlap sack full of grass and dandelions to feed the rabbits.

For our Christmas roast, we asked a neighbor to butcher one of the rabbits for the cost of fifty pennies.

In order to have room for everybody at the table, my parents set up some sawhorses with planks on the top covered by a bed sheet that served as a tablecloth.

Christmas night, my parents went to the midnight Mass and came home early in the morning. Our older brothers and sisters had to stay with us younger children and kept us in suspense telling us about the Christ child that was about to come with sweets and surprises.

The signal that the Christ child had completed his job and that he was leaving was the sound of a little bell. Then my parents came into our room and had with them new socks and for the first time new underwear for all of us.

"From the Christ child," my mother said. We had to dress in the bedroom, line up, and then we went, singing, "Oh children, come all, to the manger of Bethlehem," until we arrived at our manger, which was placed on a table in a corner. Then we surrounded the manger, where my father read the Christmas story.

During the reading, my eyes wandered sideways to our kitchen table. There was the Christmas tree with real candles brightening the room surrounded by plates with cookies and sweets for everyone. In addition, every plate had a toy or a sweater that my mother had knitted during the long nights before Christmas. Often I think about the statement the Austrian writer Peter Rossegger made once: "How rich were we at the time when we were poor."

Slowly our conditions at home turned for the better. Hitler's promise to abolish unemployment and bring Germany out of the biggest depression seemed to become reality. The economy had improved, and people who were out of work for many years suddenly were employed again. Building up Germany's infrastructure, among other things, employed many. The Autobahn was one of the biggest projects. The new organization, the National Labor Service, in which most young men over the age of seventeen had to enroll, worked on many of the projects. Some assertion in later years was that all this was the preparation for war.

Now, at least sometimes, we had a piece of meat on Sunday or even an orange for dessert. Yes, we were still poor, but it was much better then the past years.

My father, who earned a minimum on wages, tried to supplement his earnings by selling soft drinks to his coworkers at the small factory. The only problem was that he had to store the bottles at home. Once we children had a taste of the delicious beverage, we wanted more. Therefore, at the end of the month, there was not enough money to pay the supplier. My father had to give up his side job, and that was the end of the free lemonade for us.

Crystal Night: The Beginning of the End

The year was 1938. We woke up one morning and learned that during the night Hitler's SA (storm troopers) demolished all the Jewish stores in the city. Worldwide, this night was known as the "Crystal Night." To see for ourselves, some of my friends and I went to the city. What we saw was devastating. All the merchandise was lying on the street mingled with the broken glass of the shop windows. We were told that it was revenge for the killing of a German official by a Jewish individual in Paris. My mother was outraged. "The Jewish businesspeople were always there when I needed shoes for my children; they are good-hearted people." Being nine years old and seeing the brutality of this day made me sad, but when everything was built up again, the city looked normal once more. Yes, the damaged stores were intact, but the human tragedy had just begun.

It was after the war that we found out what happened to those Jews that were arrested that day. We put aside the event of the Crystal Night and lived our life. Once in a while I saw a person wearing the Star of David with the insignia "Jude." Again, I was just too young to have any further thoughts about it.

At school, we learned the story: that the Jews were the source of all the evil. They were the enemy of a prosperous Germany. They made their fortunes by deceiving the honest German worker and his family.

My parents had a different opinion. They said, "Today it's them, and tomorrow it's our turn," meaning the Catholics and Christians. In later years, when I was loathed for going to church, I remembered the words of my parents.

In 1939 my brother John still held his job as a carpenter, and Willi, after his two-year time at the National Labor Service, was drafted into the German army, the artillery. Paul, eighteen, finished his apprenticeship and was now supervisor over forty apprentices.

Gertrud, my oldest sister, twenty-one at that time, worked as a laundress at a small laundry company. During my summer vacation, it was my job to deliver her lunch. It was a long walk every day. The way I walked, it took sometimes an hour, other times one and a half hours one way, depending on what I found to investigate on my way. Therefore, when I arrived at the destination, the soup was cold and sometimes spilled, but Gertrud never complained.

When I turned ten years old, I enrolled as an altar boy. The most strenuous task for being accepted was that we had to learn all those prayers in Latin. Some of them caused more problems than others. The one I just couldn't comprehend was called the "Suscipiat." (*"Suscipiat Dominus sacrificium de manibus tuis, ad lau–*

dem ET gloriam nominis Sui, ad utilitatem quoque nostram, totiusque ecclesiae suae sanctae.")

At the Mass, celebrated in Latin, we altar boys had to kneel at the side of the priest, bow our heads, and start with the "Suscipiat." I do not know if the priest ever noticed that I was whispering some nonsense with no meaning, pretending I knew what I was praying. However, in my defense, all the other prayers were no deception.

Ringing the two large bells in the tall steeple before the service was another duty we had to fulfill. Thick, heavy ropes dangled down from the very high ceiling. We started by pulling the ropes first, slowly, until we accomplished the right rhythm. Then came fun time. With a powerful jump, we were holding on to the rope, which carried us almost to the high ceiling above. The only problem was that the large bells came out of their rhythm and were all mixed up. Of course, every time that happened, the priest knew, and it was quite often that we appeared at the service with red ears caused by the priest's punishment. Of course, we deserved it. If he would have found out that we once in a while had a little sip from his good Mass wine and then supplemented the wine with water, the punishment would have been much more severe.

After I attended the parochial school for four years, the Nazi government dissolved all parochial schools. The crosses in our classrooms were replaced with Hitler's portraits. Was this the beginning of the prosecution of Christians? It was a sad day for me. My Catholic parents were furious. I was glad for a shorter distance to school. Our new school was only twenty minutes from home instead of one hour. The readjustment was difficult at first. I lost most of my friends and some nice teachers from the Catholic school. To top all that, we had to start a new letter style. It seemed we had to start from the first grade all over again. The religious education was reduced to only one hour a week.

Nineteen thirty-nine was also the year I was sent for six weeks to a large farm near Magdeburg, located in what was later known as East Germany. It was about a day's train ride from home. My dream was to spend my summer vacation away from home and my daily chores. When we were sent to a vacation on the farm, it was also the best chance to learn about the life of a farmer. Little did we know that some of those farmers would use us as cheap labor. When we arrived at our destination, a small country rail station, we were greeted by our soon-to-be foster parents for the next six weeks. While we were waiting in a group of about twenty children—one of them was a classmate of mine—a heavy set woman came toward me. She took control of me and stated, with her harsh voice, "You come with me."

The woman was leading me out of the station to where a horse and buggy awaited us. She introduced me to the driver, one of her farmhands. My first ride with a buggy was quite a thrill but too short. After about two miles, we arrived at this miraculous farm.

The house was large and roomy. When I climbed up the stairs following the woman, I heard her groan. She had a difficult time getting up the stairs. Somehow this big woman frightened me! Finally, we came to the door of the room what I could call "my room" for six weeks. The room, perhaps modest for most people, was luxurious for me. The woman ordered me to unpack my suitcase before she left the room.

Now I had time to look around to get more familiar with my new surroundings. Walking up to the window, I could see down onto the courtyard, which was demarcated by stables and barns. While I was observing the new vicinity, I watched the farmhand, Franz, the young man that had been driving the buggy, walking toward a pigeon house located at the center of the courtyard. I observed him taking a ladder and climbing up to the little house. Then he grasped one of the many pigeons and with a brutal grip twisted the little bird's head off. I was startled and began to cry. Sitting on my bed, homesickness overcame me. The nice room did not mean anything to me anymore. I wished so much I would be home.

When I was called later that day to come down for supper, I was introduced to the farmer. While I was sitting at the table, I noticed that his wife served him the slaughtered pigeon. I thought it was disgusting and could not take my eyes off the man eating the pigeon.

The next morning I got my first assignment. The fat woman showed me a mountain of potatoes. She ordered me to sort them by size. When I realized how huge that mountain was, I thought I probably need all the six weeks to finish my task. A girl about seventeen, who was from the female labor service, helped me. During our assignment, the girl and I got to know each other. She told me that she hated the fat lady and gave me the warning to be cautious.

After we had worked for a while, Franz came by. At first, he just talked to the girl, who, from my ten-year-old perspective, was very beautiful. When I looked to the side, I noticed that Franz had his hand under her skirt. When the girl caught my surprised look, she pushed him away. A few days later when I had to get a tool out of the barn, I heard a moaning and groaning from out of the straw loft above, and I had a foggy idea what was going on.

My first chore every morning was to carry the full, heavy milk cans to the curb on the road where they were to be picked up by a dairy truck. One day, my classmate and I intended to fry some eggs on a fire. He was supposed to bring a flat can or something to fry the eggs in, and I would take care of bringing the eggs. That morning I sneaked into the chicken coop, took two eggs, and put them in my pants pocket. Just as I stepped outside, the fat woman came across the yard and reminded me to take care of the milk cans. Already forgetting that I carried the eggs in my pocket, I lifted the heavy milk can and felt at the same time the slimy substance running down my leg. After finishing my job dragging the milk cans to the curb, I sneaked to a nearby creek, washed my pants, and waited until they were dry. I was lucky that nobody found out about my mishap. Of course, we never got to fry our eggs.

The farmer also had a job as a forester. Therefore, it was no surprise that he had a fox den behind the farm. Sometimes I was allowed to feed the foxes with scraps from the slaughtered chicken.

Besides all the unpleasant memories, I remember one experience with joy. The farmer brought home a tiny abandoned fawn. My job was to feed the cute little Bambi every day with a baby bottle. After a few days, the fawn followed me wherever I went. This fawn was my best friend during the six weeks I was there. I got so used to it that I was very sad to leave my little furry friend behind. It was almost all grown-up by that time. The farmer promised me that he soon would release it back into the wild.

After six weeks, I was happy to go back home and see my old friends and family again. The sad part was that the vacation was over, and I had to go back to school.

Now that I had turned ten years old, I had the duty to join the young Hitler Youth. Some of my friends joined as soon as they turned ten years old because being a member of the Hitler Youth was required of every boy and every girl. It was an organization comparable with the Boy Scouts. We had to attend two meetings a week. At the meetings, we learned under strict discipline scouting, singing, sports, and all the things a boy at that age is interested in. After a boy turned fourteen, he had the choice to join either the flying Hitler Youth to learn how to fly a glider or join the music corps or any other of the many different interest groups of this organization.

The uniform consisted of black pants, a brown shirt with a shoulder belt, a large black scarf, and a red arm bandage with a white stripe and swastika. My desire during the time I belonged to the Hitler Youth was to have a brown shirt like all the others. Was it because we did not have the money, or was it my parents' absolute rejection of Hitler's government that my wish never became reality? I was ashamed being one of the few without a uniform and had only my normal street clothes to wear. The boys without a brown shirt always had to march on the end of the squad. It would be great to march up front beating the drums or to blow the trumpet.

We learned that the swastika, the Nazi emblem, had its origin from the old German tribes thousands of years ago celebrating the solstice. Straw was coiled around the outer rim of a spooked wheel and set ablaze. The wheel then was rolled from a hill down into the valley. When part of the rim was burned off, the swastika was originated. Since Hitler was so obsessed with the old German tribes, he adopted their emblem. It wasn't until after the war, that we found out that he made this century-old symbol the most hated one of all time.

At our meetings when we were marching through the city, we carried the Hitler Youth flag up front. It was the duty of every German citizen to greet the flag when it passed by. I observed that the Jewish people, who were easily recognized by the Star of David with the inscription "Jude" on their clothing, were the only ones that never saluted the flag. Later we were told it was the law that prohibited the Jews to salute the Nazi flag.

The exclamation of Hitler that "the German youth must be tough as leather, hard as Krupp steel, and as quick as a greyhound" followed us throughout our entire adolescence.

Our Hitler Youth leaders tried with great effort to educate about the Nazi doctrine, which could be described as brainwashing. To achieve their goal, they offered various activities to make our meetings more interesting. The activities I was most interested in were the education as a sail-flight pilot, radio operator, and shooting practices. Then there was the yearly track and field competition, where thousands participated in a large stadium. On the other side, I hated the marching exercise and learning new marching songs.

In the summer of 1939, my parents and some of my brothers and sisters visited one of my uncles. I remember all the adult talk was about the possibility of the coming war. At the end of our visit, I heard them say, "We hope we see each other again before the war starts." Our father had told us many times before how ugly World War I was. He was wounded in Flanders, France, and he watched many of his comrades get killed.

We learned in school that it was unacceptable when Poland closed the border between the German mainland and the province of East Prussia, a part of the German state. It was now only accessible from the Baltic Sea. That Polish hordes came daily over the German border, killing German civilians. The inculpation was corroborated with ghastly photographs of the killed victims. How long would Germany put up with these attacks on their innocent people? The Nazi propaganda was running full blast.

The day was September 1, 1939. I remember that Friday morning when I was on my way to school. From an open window of one of the passing houses came the loud voice over the radio. All negotiations failed, and German troops fought back and marched into Poland. World War II had started. I remembered the stories our father told us about the brutality of World War I. What would this new war bring us? Would we have to go through another misery, and how long would it last? Soon came the order that all windows needed to be darkened and all streetlights turned off so as not to give the hostile airplane a target. Cars and trucks had only small slits as their headlights. In the meantime, my friends and I were involved in another kind of war. Since I changed over to the community school, we had problems with the other classmates from our surrounding area.

I do not remember what started it all. Daily, after school, we had rock fights. The danger of losing an eye or ending up with a bloody hole in our heads did not stop us at all. Realizing the danger, some fathers took part in our fights—perhaps to stop us from getting hurt, or maybe they just wanted to be part of the occasion. Our battlefields were a few selected areas, close to where the fist-sized rocks were readily available to be used for road building. One of the battlegrounds was a large, steep meadow with a house located down in the valley. Sometimes during our encounter, a few windows were broken. That was usually the time when the occupant came out and participated in our fight.

I still remember when the father of one of our opponents chased Albert, another friend of mine. Albert lured the man who was chasing him to the steep part on the edge of the road where Albert made a quick stop and lay down. The man was not prepared, and his feet tripped over Albert's body. He landed like a spread eagle on the middle of the road. At school, sitting next to our adversary and listening to the lecture of our teacher about the dangerous games we played only increased our obsession and the continuation of our fights.

The greatest idea came to me at the time when I found this inner tube from a bicycle. Finding the right tree close to one of our battlegrounds was the easiest part. I found just the right one that had fork-like branches on the top. Within a short time, I converted the eighty-foot tree into a giant slingshot by using the inner tube. Getting a sufficient amount of big rocks up to the top was the difficult part. After completion, I waited at the top of the tree for the rock fight to start and had the proud feeling that I would be the hero of the day.

As soon as the fight started, the slingshot was loaded. It was not easy to pull the inner tube and hold on for dear life eighty feet above the ground. My anticipation reached the limit when I finally released the projectile. Surprise turned into disappointment when I saw the large rock dropping just about five feet from the trunk of the tree. I had hoped so much that I would change the strategy of all future rock fights with my new invention. My secret weapon was a disappointment. The scary part of my adventure came when I climbed down the tree and our adversaries recognized my incapacity. They took aim with all the rocks they could find. Ending up with another hole in my head and blood running down my face, I reached home. My mother again took me to the first aid man, as so many times before.

It was during our school vacation in the spring of 1940 that I was sent with a train full of other children to Bavaria. The reason again was to educate us about life on a farm and at the same time experience a vacation we otherwise could not have afforded. My best friend, Alfred, was also with me. I do not know how it happened, but at our destination, we were separated. I felt very sad about that. Things turned out okay when I found out that one of my classmates from my neighborhood was in the same village as I was. His nickname was Heinemann. He was known throughout the neighborhood and the school for the awful things he did to animals, especially frogs. We heard horror stories about

Heinemann. He inserted a straw into a frog's behind and blew the frog up like a balloon until it exploded. Another time he supposedly made little crosses and nailed the frogs on to them. I had never witnessed the cruelties he had been known for, and I certainly would not ask him since he was the only playmate I had then. His punishment came at unexpected moments, and I was not so innocent on some of the retributions.

The village was very romantic, and most buildings were from the Middle Ages. The home where I stayed was an average-sized farm. The farmer had one son by the name of Fred, twelve years of age, one year older than I was.

Soon after my arrival, I recognized that the only reason I was there was to help with the hard task of farm work. My job consisted of cleaning the cow stable and helping Fred with the harness of the cows to harvest potatoes at the nearby field. The potato field was plowed with a single plow pulled by only one cow; a horse was unaffordable. Fred and I had then to collect the exposed harvest and fill the many burlap sacks.

On one hot afternoon, I was alone at the farm until Heinemann came by for a visit. Anxiously I waited to demonstrate the new hay hoist at the barn. Although I was not allowed to use the crane, I had watched very closely to see how Fred operated that monster. That afternoon I demonstrated to Heinemann how to pick up a bundle of hay, lifting it about fifteen feet off the ground. Then I switched the control, and the crane traveled slowly to the end of the barn. I switched the control again, which opened the prongs and dropped the load onto the stored hay below. Heinemann was excited. He asked me to do the same with him.

"No problem," I said. After the crane came down, Heinemann hung on to the prongs. Slowly I lifted him into the air, hoping that he could hang on. When he was about fifteen feet off the ground, I switched the control. Then something terrible happened. I must have pushed the wrong button. Instead of sending the crane to the other side, the prongs opened, and Heinemann came sailing down and landed with his back on the hard concrete floor. He was lying there fighting for air. Scared to death, I kneeled down to his side to assist him. After what seemed an eternity, he was breathing normally again, and I helped him to get up. Thank God he was okay.

At the outskirts of the village was a huge villa belonging to a doctor. A nearby corral was the playground for six to eight horses. There was also a Shetland pony and a mule. At one of my visits at the corral, I met the doctor's daughter. She was the same age as I was, and her name was Ingrid. It was no surprise that we became good friends. We sat for hours inside the horse stable. She wanted to know everything about me while she demonstrated how to braid a horse's mane.

On one occasion, I invited Heinemann to come with me. After I introduced him to my new girlfriend, he asked her if he could ride the little Shetland pony. Even though Heinemann had never sat on a horse in his life, he assured Ingrid that this was his favored pastime. Ingrid made only one request: that he had to saddle his own horse. He agreed. After a little help from

Ingrid, he managed finally to sit proudly in the saddle. She handed him the riding whip. It needed only a soft touch with the whip, and this little animal took of as if Satan were chasing him.

When Heinemann was paying too much attention keeping his balance, he did not pay attention to the low-hanging branches of some fruit trees. Ingrid and I were first in shock when we witnessed Heinemann running into one of those branches, brushing him off the horse. Since he was wearing sandals, one of them was caught in the stirrups. The little powerful pony kept right on going, dragging the screaming Heinemann behind him. Ingrid grasped the situation first and mounted the horse next to us. Without a saddle, she managed to catch up with the racing horse and its screaming load. Heinemann was not seriously hurt but promised to never sit on a horse again.

On one occasion, I asked the doctor if I could ride the mule, which came originally from a French circus. The doctor said that he had to visit a patient of his at the next village and, if I would saddle the mule myself, I could ride with him. Therefore, I did. The doctor took a shortcut through the fields and meadows. I had a hard time keeping up with him when suddenly I was in the middle of a marshland, the mule sinking deeper and deeper into the soft, mushy ground. I was holding on to the bridle for dear life. Then the mule decided to lower his head to eat some of that green grass, and since I was still holding on to the bridle, I slid head first into the wet marsh. It seemed the mule had just waited for that moment. He pranced wildly first and then, before

I could stop him, raced the way back home and left me behind up to my knees in the marsh. This was the last time I asked the doctor to ride one of his horses.

At the farm, I still had to do my chores. One morning, I had the smelly, disgusting pleasure to fill the big tank on a wagon with the liquid manure from the cesspool. After I was almost done, Heinemann stopped by. I still do not know what came over me. When I asked him to help me to stop a leak at the cock at the end of the tank, I directed him so that he was with his face close to the spraying mechanism. Then with a quick move, I opened the cock, and within a second, he was covered with the ghastly smell of the sewage. With a loud scream, he jumped at me, and we were involved in slippery, sliding fight. The farmer came running and separated us. He also got some of the smelly substance on his clothes. He pushed us under a nearby pump, where we had to wash each other until we were clean. There were no winners at this fight.

After six weeks, we all went back home. It was the end of our summer vacation, and a few changed things awaited me at home.

The time for play and games was sharply reduced when I was assigned to deliver shoes for our cobbler. Every weekend I had to report to his small old shack located on a stream down in the valley. The shack consisted of three small rooms. The entry room, the smallest of the three, had a bunk bed with a layer of straw, which the old handyman inhabited. He was a poor homeless man and spoke most of the time in Polish. His knowledge of the German language was very limited. For various chores, such as taking care of all the chickens, rabbits, and the garden, the cobbler gave him shelter.

The interior of the main room consisted of a combination grind and polishing machine, a low table with tools, and a low chair, the cobbler's working place. Between his knees, he was holding his adjustable iron mold, on which he slipped the shoe that needed to be repaired. Also, part of the room was a potbelly stove. The stove made the room comfortable and cozy in the wintertime. There was always the smell of leather in the room.

Sometimes when I was sitting in the corner, patiently waiting for the shoes to be ready, the handyman—I always addressed him with his last name, Mr. Backer—boiled some water on the stove. He then went outside, came back with a jittery clamor of a chicken, and asked the cobbler for his approval. Then he walked out again, and shortly thereafter, he came with a headless chicken dripping blood into the room, took the water from the stove, dipped the chicken into it, and started to pull out the feathers. The leathery smell of the room was soon replaced by the stinky smell of the butchery.

When finally the last repaired shoe was filling my blue sack for the day's run, I finally escaped the distasteful smell. Outside, the cold and crisp air filled my lungs, and I went on my long journey to all those clients spread over many square miles. Some days when I was ringing the doorbell and the door opened, I could smell the mouth-watering scent of the fresh baking Sunday cake. With it came the sound of a certain ludicrous broadcast over the radio only to be heard on Saturday afternoons. It seemed so cozy; I then wished so much I could be home! Brushing my thoughts away, I swung my blue sack over my small shoulder and walked the many miles until I delivered the last pairs of shoes.

When I returned to the cobbler's shack, he gave me one more assignment. "Go down the road to the corner bar," he said, and he handed me a little flat bottle. "Tell the owner to fill it up, and tell him his shoes will be finished by next week." I did what I was asked to do and walked the mile down the road to get the cobbler's schnapps. When I came back, he gave me fifty pennies, the pay for that day, and I was on my way home. The next Saturday I would be back to make another delivery.

Arriving at home, I gave my mother the fifty pennies. The water for the weekly bath was already boiling on the large stove, and my mother filled the two feet large tin tub with soothing warm water. Oh, it felt so good after the hard day's work. While I enjoyed the warm water, I dreamed of adventures far away in space. After our bath, we all sat on our wooden bench, and my mother served us a sandwich with liver sausage and hot chocolate.

This all changed during the next few months. Since the beginning of the war in September, every family had received monthly ration stamps. At first, food allowance was still more plentiful than our small family budget could afford. The longer the war continued, the smaller the ration became. The irony was that at peacetime, we did not have the money for food and clothing. During the war when employment was in abundance, daily necessities became scarce while luxury items disappeared completely; we were rich when we were poor and poor when we were rich. There was a shortage of everything from groceries to toilet articles to clothing. The ration cards supplied only the bare essentials. Gasoline was in very short supply. Many of the trucks were outfitted with a large wood-burning kettle that produced gas from wood to power the vehicle. Even a director of a large company that lived nearby had one of those monstrous kettles mounted on the trunk of his limousine.

In the beginning, we were fortunate. One of our neighbor's daughters worked at a bread bakery. We gave her our bread ration card, and in return we received more bread than our rations allowed. The bread was a week or more old, but it helped us to overcome the ever-present hunger.

Once a week my mother and I carried the same tin tub, which also served as our bathtub, to the bakery. There they filled the tub up to the edge, and we carried the heavy load of bread the long way home. Since I was so much smaller than my mother and the tub tilted, I was required to carry the larger part of the load. As soon as we got home, Mother treated me with a sandwich that consisted of one side with margarine and the other side with molasses. I would treat myself by eating first the slice with the molasses, which did not taste so good, but when I got to the side with the margarine that had some of the molasses on it, that was a delicacy.

At times, I was amazed the way my mother stretched the little food we had. When I asked her once why she always put the spreading on the short side of the bread—the bread had a tapered shape—my mother answered, "Because it uses up less spreading."

At the beginning of the war, there were no more coffee beans; the coffee consisted of malted coffee with some coffee beans mixed in. It was our task as children to pick out the coffee beans. Then Mother handed us the coffee mill, and after the coffee was ground, Mother invited a neighbor woman, who also was a mother of eleven children, and the two enjoyed a real cup of coffee.

My brother Willi was now at the western front fighting in France. Daily special bulletins came over the radio about the swift actions of the German army driving the French far over the Maginot Line. When finally the newscast came that German troops marched without fighting into Paris, we all thought the war would be over. We received a letter from Willi that he was well and healthy and might soon be coming home on furlough.

Our dream about the end of the war was shattered when John was drafted into the army. Before John left, he gave me the order to transport his large four feet long toolbox from our house to his apartment. Since he'd married, he moved with his wife, Clara, about eight miles away. A nearby company that fabricated coffins had a two-wheel cart to transport the coffins. The wheels of the handcart were about four feet in diameter, which made the loading platform high off the ground, almost to the height of myself. After I came back with the borrowed cart, John and a neighbor lifted the heavy toolbox onto the cart. The most difficult test for me was to keep the balance. While I left home to transport the toolbox to John's new apartment, I knew that this was the greatest challenge and, at the same time, the hardest job I had ever tackled in my short life. Our city was located high on a hill while we lived on the outskirts down in the valley. Pushing the big cart with the heavy load up the hill over cobblestone roads was almost too much. Before the day was over, I had my most difficult task completed.

War with Russia

John had been gone only a few months when in June 1941, the special bulletin came over the radio that German troops were marching against Russia. It seemed that the hope for the end of the war was now lost.

It was a very foggy day in November of the same year when Paul, the last of my brothers, had to leave home. He too had to join the army. I will never forget when we said good-bye to Paul. He was wearing his fishbone pattern winter coat. While he walked down the road, we stood at the front door until he disappeared into the dense fog.

I always admired Paul for his intelligence, his accomplishment in gymnastics, and mostly his high moral standards. He was highly respected by everyone he met. It came as no surprise that his army superiors immediately recognized his intelligence and his competence. After his basic training, he was asked to participate in a training course to be an officer. Paul nor any of our family ever adored the Nazi doctrine, but even John, with his underground work at the "Travelers of the Cross," said before he left: "I am called to do my duty, and I will do my best, as I would do any other duty."

After about one and a half years, Paul was promoted to lieutenant. This was unusual. At that time, it was almost impossible to get into an officer rank without graduating at least from high school. We did not have the money for any of us to go to high school, but every one of us learned a trade.

My Brother John, Willi, Paul and myself

While John and Paul were stationed in France, Willi was on the Russian front. His letters sometimes were very disturbing. In one letter, he reported that he was twenty miles from Moscow and could see the streetcars in the city.

His most dreadful letter we received in early 1942. He stated in his letter:

> I will never in my life forget my twenty-fifth birthday, November 18, 1941. A surprise attack by the Russians drove us back a few miles, leaving behind the small field

hospital we maintained in a farmer's barn with over one hundred wounded comrades. The next day we started our counteroffensive; we conquered the territory we lost the day before. We made a ghastly discovery. The barn, our field hospital, was burned down, and with it, all of the wounded, except for some of them, were crucified to the barn doors. On many of them, the ring fingers with wedding rings and some their genitals were cut off. The Russians made sure that none of the wounded survived.

Our worries about our loved ones in uniform increased immensely. Mother prayed every day for their safe return and for the end of this brutal war.

Willi spent the rest of the war on the Russian front. Paul and John joined him later. However, they were stationed in a different part of Russia. Franzi, at seventeen, had to enter the women's labor service. From the nine of us children, five were still at home. Our family was shrinking.

Cloister Roggenburg

At the age of thirteen, I was sent for six months to a camp in Bavaria. Those camps were designated for children to escape the daily bombing of the German cities in the north by the Allies. Many of my classmates and friends were sent to different parts of Bavaria and to the far eastern part of Germany. The camps were separated into girls' and boys' camps and had a timeline of six months. Our camp was at on old convent that was more than two hundred years old.

It was mostly a happy time, but there were also some sad times. As soon as we arrived, we received a large burlap sack and were ordered to fill our sack with straw from the adjacent barn. Since I knew this was my sleeping mattress, I filled my sack until it was plump and round. After all, I wanted to have a soft mattress to sleep on. Our sleeping room was a large hall with about fifty bunk beds. I picked one of the upper bunks. Everyone received two blankets for bedding. When I went to bed that night, I hoped that the plump-filled sack would subside once I lay on it. The surprise came during the night when during my sleep I suddenly plunged down to the ground. Before the next night, I went back to the barn and unloaded half of the straw. From then on, my nights were more pleasant.

The monastery was located at the most picturesque region of Bavaria. Large buildings surrounded the beautiful baroque twin tower church that was constructed in 1722.

Cloister Roggenburg

Located on the south end of the complex were the stables with cows and other farm animals. To the west were the large buildings that housed a restaurant, serving as our dining room. Located upstairs was one large room, our leisure room.

Adjacent was the large sleeping room with our bunk beds. At the rear of the building was a small outside bowling

Cloister Roggenburg, our quarter

lane. The surrounding farmers came here on Sunday afternoons to indulge in some games. In addition, an old building housed an elevator that was maybe two hundred years old. The elevator was nothing more than a large, deep hole at one corner of the building with a wooden platform. At the center of the otherwise empty building was a big, round vertical wooden post anchored at the roof and the dirt floor. A chain led from the post to the corner of the building into the dark elevator shaft, where it was attached to the platform. Anchored to the vertical post was a horizontal bar about fifteen feet in length and three feet from the ground. This bar was the driving mechanism for the elevator. A horse, harnessed to the bar, was guided in a circular motion around the center post. The chain winding around the top of the center post would then lift or lower the elevator depending on if the horse would go clockwise or counterclockwise.

Surrounding the complex was a large apple orchard. This orchard was off limits to us, and so was the old elevator building. Our camp leader, who was responsible for our welfare, was very strict and served as our schoolteacher. His assistant, a seventeen-year-old leader of the Hitler Youth, had the responsibility for our outdoor activities.

I cannot explain the aversion the camp leader had toward me. His dislike elevated at certain times into torture. I remember one occasion. Our washroom had a long row of faucets with one large basin. Every Saturday was bathing time. We all had to go into the washroom nude and had to wash ourselves from top to bottom. There was only cold water, of course, and no heat in the wintertime.

It was one day in fall when the camp leader came storming into the washroom with a stick in his hand. Making his way through the naked bodies of the other boys, he was aiming at me as the target, accusing me of stealing apples from the orchard. Before I could defend myself, the stick he was carrying whistled through the air, hitting my naked body time after time. Crying out and asserting that I was innocent did not help. Yes, I had done many forbidden things, but this time I was innocent. The hurt and the inhumanity in the presence of all the other boys made me swear that someday, when I was grown up, I would pay him back.

Down in the valley, surrounded by tall spruce trees, was a dreamlike, picturesque, large lake. The wintertime presented us with many joyous activities. Any free time we had we spent down on the lake. Some of the boys had ice skates. We exchanged the skates so everyone had a chance to skate. We cut sticks from the trees to play our favorite game: hockey.

One day we had the idea to build an ice racer. We organized three posts from a fence and laid them out into a triangle. Then we covered them with some wooden boards, mounting one skate up front and two on each side at the rear. A blanket tightened to a vertical post as a sail completed the handsome rig. As soon as the wind was just right, three of us jumped onto the rig. The racer started slowly at first, picking up speed gradually. When we reached the middle of the lake, the speed was at the peak. As we raced toward the shore, we realized that we did not include in our design how to stop or turn this thing. We decided to jump, one at a time. Since I was the last one to slide off, the weight of only me could not keep the racer on the ice. I felt a tremendous power swirling me through the air while the rig landed on my body. Luckily, I escaped with minor bruises.

The thick ice of the lake also served a very practical purpose. As for generations before, the workers of the convent went to the lake with horses pulling a sleigh. Armed with six feet long saws, they cut large sections out of the ice. Those sections were like large rafts. After this was completed, the ice rafts were cut into blocks of ice and carried to the sleigh. The horses had to work very hard to pull the load up the hill to the convent where the ice blocks were carried into the shed, where the elevator was located. The horse then was harnessed on to the horizontal post and the ice blocks lowered down.

For the first time, a few of us went with one of the workers through a large door and down countless steps deep underground. Finally, we reached the point where the elevator was resting with the heavy load. To one side, there was another door leading into a large room where the ice was to be stored. When we entered the room, there was still ice that had been stored the year before. The cool temperature underground and the sawdust used to cover the ice kept it solid for a long time.

While we were so far down underground, we discovered a tunnel approximately two feet wide by four feet high. We wanted to find out where this tunnel would lead. We were told that the tunnel was ending far away in the forest as a getaway in times of war or pursuit.

Since the workers did not let us find out by ourselves where the tunnel was ending, we had to find another way. One afternoon six of us sneaked into the forbidden shed. We decided that three of us would operate the elevator while the other three stepped onto the platform and would be slowly lowered to the ground level. At a signal from there, we would bring the elevator up again to take turns.

One of the boys and I operated the horizontal post. The third one that remained with us decided he would rather stand on the horizontal bar and hold on to the vertical post. I do not know what went wrong. As soon as we put the elevator into motion, the fifteen-foot pole was too difficult to hold back due to the load on the elevator platform. When my helper let go, it was impossible for me to hold on. I lay with my belly on the post and let it carry me around in the circle. When the speed picked up like an orbiter used at the space program training, I jumped off and lay flat on the ground, making sure the post didn't hit me the next time around.

From the ground, I was able to observe my partner at the center post. As he was holding on for dear life, I saw his feet losing ground, and his body lifted slowly into a horizontal position. His hands were still holding on to the post, until the gravity force got too strong. I observed his body flying through the air, and he was thrown against the wall; then he fell to the ground and seemed lifeless.

The big crashing noise of the elevator platform hitting the bottom of the shaft added another worry. Did they, down there, survive the crash? As soon as everything was quiet, my other partner and I went to the boy on the ground. He was unconscious. We screamed down the shaft. From far down came the answer that they were okay. After a while, the unconscious friend of ours was starting to breathe, fighting for air. It seamed to take forever until he was okay. We were able to open the door that was leading underground. When we found the others, we were glad no one was hurt. We promised not to tell anyone what happened. The consequences would have been heavy punishment.

It was close to Christmas. The year was 1942. It was at the middle of the war, and there was a shortage of almost everything. We at the camp decided to start toy manufacturing. We organized lumber from surrounding carpenters. Soon our leisure room turned into a large Christmas workshop. We turned out so many different toys, and we were looking forward to the day when all the farmers' children found one of our gifts under the Christmas tree. There were trains and trucks, the badger dog that wiggled his whole body, and even chess games with every chessman artistically carved.

As a gesture for our gifts to the surrounding children, each of the farmers invited one of us to celebrate Christmas day with them, every one of us with a different family. This helped us to overcome our homesickness during that time. While we all felt fairly safe about the Allied bombing, we listened every day to the radio. The bombing of the German cities had intensified. Almost every day there was news that the Allied bombing had destroyed another city.

We all worried about our loved ones at home, but so far my hometown had been spared. Then came the day when one of the higher leaders of the Hitler Youth came to the camp. His message was very sad. The family of one of my friends perished in an air attack by the Allies on the city of Duisburg. "They died for great Germany and our Fuehrer," the leader stated to the boy to calm him down.

The day finally came that, not long after Christmas, we went back home. The long ride on the train was accompanied by a surprise. Our camp director, who tortured me most of the time, turned suddenly into a lamb. He treated me with the highest regard. As the only one, he asked me if I wanted to sleep in the suitcase net above our seats.

The reunion at home was joyful but also sad. Maria, four years older than I was, also had to leave home. She had been drafted into the antiaircraft corps. Franzi, who served at the women's labor corps, automatically transferred into the army.

I received a letter from the highest leaders in the Hitler Youth to participate in a test to be enrolled into the Adolf Hitler School. To attend this school, was the highest honor given to a member of the Hitler Youth. The purpose was to train future officers. My first reaction was a proud feeling for being the only one selected from all my friends. I also was scared taking this test, knowing my academic limits. It was my mother who convinced me that it was just another way to recruit more cannon feed, and she was not willing to sacrifice another child. As soon as my mother read the letter, she was furious. She tore the letter up and burned it. My father agreed with my mother but was more concerned about the consequences. For the next few weeks, long after the requested report date, I was worried what they would do to my mother or me. Thank God there was no retribution.

The weekly meetings with the Hitler Youth became increasingly boring. My dream of being a sail-plane pilot did not materialize. Since I had no uniform, I was pushed to the end of the line and mostly was assigned to a marching group. I hated this.

Suddenly things were spiced up with free tickets for the movie theater. The catch: the movies were shown Sunday mornings, and everyone was ordered to attend. My parents were outraged since Sunday morning was our time to attend church service. I myself was looking forward to going to the movies. The only movie I had ever seen was an Indian movie starring Shirley Temple. Besides, I found, as any boy at my age would, that a movie was much more exciting than the boring Mass on Sunday morning.

Of all the movies we had to attend, the one that had the largest impact on me was the movie *My Life for Ireland*. It was about the life of a freedom fighter against the English. Other movies followed, and I remember the titles: *Jew Seuss*, with my favorite actor, Kristin Soederbaum; then there was the movie *The Eternal Jew*. The hate movies against the Jewish race left no impact on us. They were nothing but a poorly made propaganda campaign against the Jews, who were compared with rats. They were so disgusting and exaggerated that not one of us who witnessed the actions on the movie screen would believe what we were told. The movies compared the Jewish population with the most hated animals, the rats that spread disease and deceitfulness throughout the German population. They were portrayed as devious rapists with no morals who achieved their wealth through swindling and corruption.

Back at my school, I was selected to take a course to be a gymnastics coach for my school, although my academic achievements needed much to be desired.

One day on my way home from school, a little girl started to dance around me with the honest brutality children sometimes display. She was singing with her innocent voice, "Your brother is dead; your brother is dead." Not understanding her abnormal behavior, I continued on my way home. There, my weeping mother greeted me. With her crying voice, she told me that John would never come home again. He was killed at one of the most horrible battlegrounds of World War II: Stalingrad. His daughter, only one year old, would never know her father, who was an example of a human being who wanted to make the world a better place. He did what he had to do. When John left home, he said to my mother, "All my life I tried to do what is right. Now it is my duty not to exclude myself. I could not live with myself thinking someone else's mother would grieve over her son just because I despise this system. I will do what I am called to do." Until my mother passed away, she always believed that the Nazis killed John and that they may have found out about his activity at the underground organization the Travelers of the Cross. We all were shocked at first when we realized that we would never see John again, and we were overcome with grief. This grief turned into hate for those responsible for John's death. His wife would never be with him, and he would never experience fatherhood with the one-year-old daughter he loved so much. His wife loved John, and she never remarried.

I continued to report twice a week at the meetings of the Hitler Youth. On a hot, early summer day, I decided not to attend the meeting. I went to a local pond instead and went swimming. As I had fun swimming with a few friends, we noticed a squad of Hitler Youth coming toward us. The leader of the squad was very angry with me for not showing up at the meeting. He gave me the warning that the next time I would have to take the consequences of severe punishment. He immediately ordered me to join the group. We marched to a nearby forest. There we sat in a circle and learned some new boring songs.

Our yearly track and field sport event was canceled. The activity of Allied fighter planes had increased dramatically. The danger of having three thousand boys and girls at an open stadium was too high of a risk.

On April 1, 1943, at just fourteen years old, I was enrolled in an apprentice program as a tool and die maker. It was at the same factory at which my brother Paul was the training supervisor before he joined the army. Here again, the outstanding qualities of my brother haunted me. I just could not measure up to the achievements of my brother. Everyone expected that I would be as clever as him. I never was angry with my brother because he was so much better than me. On the contrary, I was very proud of him. Being a top gymnast was the only good quality I shared with my brother. My trainers had high hopes that I would, with the right training, make it to the Olympics. At any event I entered, I was given the top honor.

The air raids against the civilian population were dramatically increased and moved frighteningly close to our town. The promise of a *Vergeltungs Waffe*, meaning "weapon of retaliation," later known as "V 1" and "V 2" was still more than a year away. The terrible sound of the sirens three or four

As a gymnast

times at night and day was now a part of our lives. The first reaction was always tuning to a certain wavelength on the radio, indicated by the loud ticking noise of the air raid warning system. The ticking noise, periodically interrupted by a female voice, gave information about the path of the hostile bomb squadrons. The American B-17 carried out the day aggression while the night attacks belonged to the RAF.

At the beginning of the bombing, everyone fled hastily into the shelters. After a while I got used to it, and I often skipped the run to the shelter. I was just too tired and hoped for the best. Our protections were the two basements of our house. Each of the basements was located opposite of the large building. One shelter was an arch-like construction from large rocks and considered quite safe against small bombs. The other one, which our family was assigned to, was exactly the opposite. It was practically a large room on the lowest floor. In one corner of the room, we managed to store an old mattress where some of the children could continue their sleep during the alert.

One of my duties as a member of the Hitler Youth was to rush immediately after an aggression to the bombing sites to retrieve casualties and help the victims salvage what remained from their personal belongings. All men of seventeen to about fifty served in the army. Some soldiers who came home on leave and went through an air raid made statements that they rather would be on the front lines fighting the enemy than experience another bomb attack in the city.

The Hell of Phosphorus Bombs

We at home had to deal with the daily bombing of the cities around us. The first bombing started May 11, 1940, about forty miles from our town. May 13, 1942, was the first large-scale carpet-bombing on the city of Cologne, twenty miles away, ever so close to our hometown. More than one thousand planes of the Royal Air Force participated. From a distance, the sky was blood red, the sign that the city was on fire. Then we heard the rumbling noise of large bombs hailing down on the city.

After one and a half hours, everything was quiet. The only sound was some lost "hero" trying to get back to his station in England. The sky was on fire until it seemed that the daylight extinguished the torment. The thousand airplanes had not destroyed the total city; more attacks would follow until the city was 90 percent ruined.

Ever since the first bombing of a German city, Mönchengladbach, the scare of being the next victim was on everyone's mind. This scare increased with the atrocious bombing of Cologne. Eventually almost all of Germany's larger cities and many small ones were bombed.

May 30, 1943, was the day when the so-called terror bombing came close to home. The air raid warning system announced that a large hostile formation was approaching the city of Wuppertal, our neighbor city only seven miles away. Shortly thereafter, the city was declared as the likely target.

Wuppertal had a population of about four hundred and fifty thousand. The city itself was located in a deep valley and divided by the river Wupper, which gave the city its name. The outskirts spread for many square miles uphill on both sides of the valley.

The thick plank that was leading from the attic window of our high-rise home toward the chimney and used by the chimney cleaner was for me the ideal observation point. Not telling anyone, I sneaked up to the attic and crawled through the small window onto the plank. For some it would have been scary being that high off the ground, especially at night, but I was never bothered by heights. I took my position on the roof on the night of May 30, 1943, after Wuppertal was declared as the target.

The roaring sound of the approaching Vickers Wellington bombing squads filled the otherwise quiet night. At a distance, the target flares hovered over the city of Wuppertal. Before the flares—we named them Christmas trees—could hit the ground, they were overpowered by the lighting inferno of the incendiary and phosphorous bombs raining down onto the city. Minutes later, the air was filled with the loud explosions of thousands of large bombs mixed with the bursting projectiles of the despaired German antiaircraft defense. By now, the horizon had turned bloody red.

The danger of being hit by shrapnel made me withdraw from my observation point. After about one and a half hours of constant carpet-bombing, only the late explosion of some scattered bombs interrupted the now quiet night.

Two of my friends and I took off and went to the badly desecrated city to help with the salvage of belongings and the rescue of the victims. After an hour, we reached the outskirts of the city. It was also the end of the line. There was no way to get any farther. The fire and the smoke were almost unbearable. The smell of burning flesh was a disgusting experience we'd never had before. There were bodies burned black, like a burned-out log from an extinguished fireplace. Others were laying there as their skin was pulled off from their bodies, skinless and red and purple in color. During the attack, some people had been in flames from the phosphorus bombs. In their agony, they jumped into the river as living torches and came out of the river, their tortured flesh still burning. The water could not extinguish the flames. At one house, a team of survivors was digging to free people buried in their basement. We helped as much as we could to salvage as much as possible from the demolished homes. In most cases, it did not amount to a lot because there was not much left.

Again I remembered my father's war stories. Those stories seemed like fairy tales compared to what we experienced. He told us about dead and wounded soldiers, but this was the deliberate murder of innocent women and children. I was just disgusted. When would all this happen to my city? When would we be the target? There was not one case of looting since any plunderer was to be shot on the spot. I am still amazed how little fear we had to walk into those houses that were ready to collapse at any time.

The outskirt of Wuppertal was no different. There was this little girl, twelve years of age, standing at a totally destroyed house. Her stone-like face showed no signs of tears. She was still in shock. Her eyes focused onto a gray-haired scalp in the ruins—the scalp of her mother. But what did happen to her fourteen-year-old brother? She found only a part of her seven-year-old sister. There were no other remains that she could identify. They all were buried in a mass grave with hundreds of others.

Not much was found of the thirteen women and children that lived there. The large, explosive bomb hit the house; they had no chance. The whole suburb was destroyed, but the military barracks not far away had no damage at all.

Many years later, I found out the whole story. During the attack, the girl's older brother was sent upstairs to get the ration cards, which his mother forgot. While he was on the second floor, the bomb hit the shelter of the house from an angle. He was thrown across the street, critically wounded, and miraculously was the only survivor from that house. The girl was babysitting that night a few miles away. Her father was assigned to the air raid protection at his workplace, a large rubber company. There was no damage to the factory. I found out that her father had a nervous breakdown. He dragged the girl every night to the cemetery to be with him when he was standing there staring at the mass grave until late at night, not knowing what was left of his loved ones since identification was impossible.

During the length of the war, I had seen a few occasional bombing damages. That morning after seeing the senseless killing of so many women and children, I was full of hate. I hated the people that were responsible for so much grief. The leaflets dropped from the Allied airplanes—meant to enlighten us about the good intention of the Allies and the wrongdoing of the Nazi government—were like a mockery. Was the murder of innocent women and children our liberation from an evil system?

I remember the cover of a Nazi oriented magazine (*Der Stürmer*). It showed a black U.S. soldier holding a knife in his mouth and pointing his machine gun toward the reader. The written text stated: "Mercy be with us if those hordes would overrun Germany. They will rape every woman and kill every German man, woman, and child in their path." My experiences during those senseless, systematic killings and the memory of my brother's letter about the event on his twenty-fifth birthday in Russia left no doubt in my mind about the Nazi version about the intention of the Allies.

As I mentioned before, Wuppertal was located in a deep valley. Standing high up on the hill, we had a good view of the large city. We observed the destruction and noticed that only one half of the city was totally destroyed, while the rest of the city was almost intact. This would all change very soon.

After the sirens screamed into the night three weeks later, the air raid warning announced that a large British bombing squadron was approaching Wuppertal. Shortly after the announcement, we sighted the flares, only this time in the direction of that part of the city that was still intact. The flares did not make it all the way to the ground when we witnessed a replica from before. Again, we went on our way to the place of horror, only this time we left during the aggression better prepared and knew what awaited us. It was the same ghastly picture as three weeks before, only this time we saw more burned bodies. On our long journey home, we passed some meadows where a scattered cowherd was also the victim of the attack.

Not all incendiary bombs ignited. On our way home, we found quite a few of them sticking into the soft soil. We collected some of them and carried them under our arms. As we passed a German military post, a soldier stopped us and asked what we were doing with those bombs under our arms. We told him that we just found them and would deliver them to the authorities at the next collection center. He ordered us to put them on the ground. Then he and another soldier grabbed one after another and with an artistic swinging motion smashed one after the other on the street, where they ignited. We watched very closely how it was done. Satisfied, we left the scene only to collect some more bombs and make our own fireworks.

Heinz, the friend that was holding my legs when I took those pictures from the bridge, had a nature call, excused himself, and went into the bushes. After a while of waiting, I sneaked up on him and with a surprise smashed one of the incendiary bombs right in font of him the way the soldiers demonstrated. I knew then that it was mean, although the bomb did not ignite on the soft ground, but I could not help to create the most comical scene: seeing him running with his pants down to his knees and his bare buttocks for everyone to see. I'm glad the incident did not happen before he held my legs at the bridge.

On the way home, we found a phosphorus bomb that had not exploded. The bomb was approximately twenty inches long, had a diameter of approximately six inches, and was orange in color.

We brought this bomb on a high nearby rock and let it then fall down. The explosion was gigantic; the whole surrounding area was in flames. We were so surprised from the effect that we started to tremble. It was mind-blowing.

Going back to work the next day, I delivered some of the leaflets we collected the day before to one of our overseers, a member of the Nazi party who was never seen without his Nazi uniform. He was not responsible for our technical training but to indoctrinate the Nazi ideas. When he asked me if I read any of the contents, I certainly denied. It was forbidden under the threat of severe penalty to read the leaflets or discuss the contents of it with another person. He gave me a lecture over the poisonous tactics of the Allies through those leaflets. He also gave me another warning, a warning that we had heard many times before: never to pick up any fountain pens. Those were highly explosive concealed booby traps targeted at children and were dropped from the Allied planes.

This high-ranking Nazi was also in charge for the well-being of about forty Russian girls and as many Polish girls that were part of the forced labor camp located on the company's ground. All the Russian girls were students and spoke excellent German, in contrast to the Polish girls who did not speak the German language at all. All the girls were treated very well. Their pay was the same as that of the German workers, and their meals at the cafeteria were the same as that of any other employee. At the many discussions I had with them, it was obvious that they all regretted being away from home and the confinement of the camp itself. It was therefore no surprise that some of them took their chance to escape the strict confinement. We all worked at the same building where I absolved my apprenticeship and there was no restriction. Having a conversation with them was no different than with any other work colleague. Some of the girls were very talkative, while others kept to themselves and would not talk to us.

Tina was, in my early teen mind, one of the most beautiful girls, with her slender body crowned by her dark hair reaching almost to her hips. She was always in very high spirits, until one morning when I came to work and saw her weeping face. I was astonished by the change in her personality and of her appearance. Her beautiful, dark hair was roughly cut to just a few inches. She explained that the night before she tried to run away but was captured. With tears running down her beautiful cheeks, she said that she was beaten and her hair cut off to discourage her and others from escaping again.

The most conversations I had were with Katja. She was seventeen years old. I was only fourteen. I felt the signs of love. Just talking to her made my blood shoot into my face.

Then there was Vera. After an accident injuring her hand, I was ordered to accompany her to the hospital. On our way, we passed a display window of a store. Since there was not much to display during the war, the business owner utilized the space with Hitler's photograph. Vera walked up to the window. Enthusiastically she started to curse Hitler's image, first in German, and after she ran out of German curses, she switched to Russian. My plea to stop her was like talking to a blank wall. In addition, my warning that someone witnessing the blasphemes of the Fuehrer might take her away did not help. Only after she apparently ran out of curses did she stop and come willingly with me to the hospital. On our way, we had a long discussion about the wickedness of the Nazis.

Vera was a type like Ann Margaret. It seemed that Vera's mission was to turn on all the male workers at the factory. On sunny summer days when it was her turn to work the late shift, she would lie with her two-piece swimsuit on the grassy meadow bordering the building. She made sure she was seen from every window of the building. Almost every worker walked up to the window to observe her.

On one occasion, during an air raid, another apprentice and I were sitting next to her at the shelter. During our conversation, she tried jokingly to tell us that she was without a navel. To prove her point, she invited us to go with her to the back room, where she would show us the evidence. Of course, we declined with great regret. Sure, we were inquisitive, but there was the law not to get friendly with laborers of a hostile country.

Our Nazi superior was trapped into a sexual romance with Vera. It all started one day when he checked the girls' quarters. When he opened the door, he found only Vera present, who immediately realized that her time had come to degrade one of the persons she hated the most. After a short conversation, Vera approached him and slowly stripped off her clothing. Then she invited him over to her primitive bed. He had always lusted after her with the same strong feelings as every other man she met. Her action was flamed by her despise of the Nazi regime and everyone that was associated with it. She knew then when he could not control himself anymore and used her seductive body as the tool to destroy him.

After the incident, Vera made sure that everyone at the company found out about the encounter. It was therefore no surprise that the Nazi authorities were informed about the incident. An official bulletin was published that the superior violated the racial laws of the government and soiled the purity of the German race. He was therefore dishonored and sent to jail, where he remained until the end of the war in 1945. His successor told me the exact happening of the incident.

Besides our technical and academic program, our daily gymnastic training was also part of our apprentice program. Every morning after raising the Nazi flag, we began our highly disciplined gymnastic hour. Weather permitting, we ran down to the valley and through the surrounding forests. My best friend at the training center was Bruno Scheongen.

On the day of July 30, 1943, we decided to go swimming at night. He came with his bike from the city, where he lived, to my favorite swimming hole down in the valley. We had a good time that night. On our way home, I placed my bath towel and shorts on his bike. As we reached my home, we said good-bye, and Bruno said, "See you tomorrow." But tomorrow never came for one of us.

After the constant warning of the screaming sirens, which went on every night for years, I was overtaken by apathy. Getting up three to four times at night was wearing me down. After a while, my family went to the shelter while I just slept through and hoped that nothing would happen during the night. All neighboring cities were in ashes, destroyed, except Solingen with about the same population as our city, about one hundred and thirty thousand.

The night of July 30 was like any other night with the usual air raid warning and shortly after the monotonous sound of the approaching hostile planes. I was tired and just wanted to sleep. Suddenly my mother came into the room and shouted, "The Christmas trees are over the city; get into the basement!" That meant that this time our city was picked as the target.

Dressed within seconds and hastening outside, I observed the last flares hovering over our city. The first incendiary bombs started to hit the ground. I became scared and ran for the shelter. One wave after another of the hostile planes came closer toward Remscheid, my hometown, to unload the deadly load. On my way to the shelter, I noticed that one bomb started to set fire to the roof of the small factory across the street. It was the factory of my friend Egon's parents. I realized if I did not react immediately, the building would burn down. With little effort, I managed to climb up onto the roof. I was just on time to pull the hexagon-shaped bomb out. With a powerful swing, I was able to get rid of the bomb and extinguished the small area that started to burn.

Continuing my way to the shelter, I observed that another neighbor's house was also on fire. I entered the basement begging for help. There was no response from the adults. One man suggested that someone should run to the next location a half-mile away where the hand-pulled fire wagon was located. Since nobody volunteered, I went on my way and ran for help.

Running frightened down the cobblestone road, I heard more incendiary bombs hitting the ground all around me. When I suddenly heard the loud screaming sound of a large, exploding bomb, I threw myself onto the ground. The almost ear-deafening sound of the explosion and shortly after the velocity of the increasing wind was the evidence that it was very close. Now running for my life, I finally reached the shelter where the fire wagon was stationed. Hastily I asked the men for help. They refused to come with me and wanted to wait until after the attack. On my way back, empty-handed, I was amazed about one of the bombing planes captured in a bundle of searchlights. The German anti-aircraft tried to give the plane the deathblow. I did not have the patience or the courage to wait for the result.

As I returned, I saw the flaming roof of the house across the street, belonging to the old man that always drilled the hole for our go-karts. Some of the men from our shelter were trying to save the household items. I went there to help, retrieving the things that were handed through the windows. In my eagerness, I was not paying attention to the couch that was dropped from the second-floor window. First I had the feeling that I was hit by one of the bombs that were still exploding around us. Only knocked out for a few seconds, I found that I was not seriously hurt and continued the salvage.

After I found out that our house was also hit by one of the incendiary bombs but was successfully extinguished, my friend Alfred, my sister Gertrud, and I went to another burning house, a villa, just a few blocks away. After saving a few household goods, we finally had to give up. The flames surrounding us were too intense, and the villa collapsed.

Now that the attack had stopped, the sky was filled with blood-red smoking clouds. The summer morning sun tried to break through the thick smoke, successful only for seconds, as if the clouds were ashamed to reveal the bloody, scorched city. For a fraction, the sun, stronger now, showed itself (in a color I cannot describe) as I had never seen it before or at any time after that morning.

Despite the fact that our hair was scorched and our bodies limp and aching, we went on our way, trying to make our way to the city. Although on the way, we were told many times that it was impossible to get there. After we had taken many detours, we finally reached the city. The ghastly panorama that awaited us was more gruesome than expected. The smell of burned human flesh was almost unbearable. The first dead bodies we encountered were fifteen girls from a Russian labor camp identified by their typical uniforms.

At one house that was hit by a heavy bomb, rescue workers could only retrieve the body parts of the victims and placed them into a tin tub, which was identical with the one we used as a bathtub when we were little, the one my mother and I used to carry the bread home. Now this tub was the temporary resting place of various legs arms and other body parts.

The smoke and heat was so intense that when we came closer to the city, we were gasping for air. We tried to get some oxygen close to the ground surrounded by screaming victims of this holocaust.

The flames of the burning houses on both sides of the street were now united as a large flaming ocean and made our advance impossible. My guilt for not trying harder will always follow me.

This is exactly the point we reached after the attack, as described in a prior paragraph. Visible in the background the destroyed town hall, only one hundred meters from the place where my aunt Maria burned to death. Photo, Historic Archive department, Remscheid.

I did not realize that only a few blocks away my uncle, without success, tried to remove a block of bricks that jammed the entry of a burning basement. Inside the inferno, thirteen people were screaming for their lives, one of them my aunt Maria, my father's sister. The gruesome discovery a few hours later just showed some unrecognizable, black, burned mass. Identification was impossible.

My aunt Maria lived by herself since my grandmother had died four years earlier. At the beginning of the war, they both lived for a while with us at home.

Since we lived on the outskirts of the city, they felt safer living with us. When I found another aunt of mine lying on the street, her skin color blue, I knew that her lungs were torn by a nearby explosion of a large bomb, called an air mine. This was next to the phosphorous bomb, the most horrendous killing weapon.

The aggression lasted fifty-eight minutes. I wanted to scream to those fleeing planes, "Can't you see from up there what you, with a push of a button, have created?"

The 243 bombers of the British Royal Air Force accomplished an outstanding job. From the 1,400 buildings, 1,100 were destroyed, and thousands of women and children perished. A few days later I found out that Bruno Schoentgen, my swimming partner from the night before, also was one of the victims. At the burial for the casualties that I attended, we were faced with some large mass graves, covered with plenty of lime to keep the smell and the spreading of disease to a minimum.

In other parts of the country with communication still intact, the following bulletin was published: "The headquarters of the German army reports: Hostile planes attacked during the day yesterday the city of Kassel. In addition, other cities occupying German territory came under attack. The city of Remscheid was attacked last night. All cities had casualties. Mass destruction and fire damage was especially heavy in the civilian part of Remscheid."

A few days after the attack, most of the dead were buried. We were ordered by the Hitler Youth to clean up the bricks of the demolished buildings. We worked side by side with many of the local women who were drafted for the hard and monotonous job. At first, we played along, but after a while, the job was dreary, and we slowly sneaked from the hard and dirty job. If someone would have looked for us, they probably would find us at our favorite swimming hole. It was so much more pleasant on a hot summer day than cleaning up old bricks.

My uncle, who had tried so hard to free the thirteen people, was the only person from all my relatives that was an official member of the Nazi party. The dispute with my father and other relatives did not change his way of thinking. Only the night of horror changed his mind. He turned against the Nazi party, and suddenly, a few days afterward, he disappeared. No one knew his whereabouts, not his daughter or his son. It was not until after the war ended that we were notified that he had died in the concentration camp of Sachsenhausen. His revolt against the Nazi system cost him his life.

After the aggression against my hometown, only one city was still intact, and that city was Solingen. This city was known for their industry of tableware, knives, and razorblades. Since our city was destroyed and the necessities of everyday life were scarce, we went sometimes on weekends to the undamaged city, hunting for things we needed.

This also came to an abrupt halt when, on Saturday afternoon, October 4, 1944, just before our weekly trip to Solingen, the air-warning sirens sounded. The loud, monotone ticking noise of the air raid warning system was occasionally interrupted by the familiar female voice announcing the approach of a large group of hostile planes. As soon as I took my position at my usual observation point on the roof of our house, I could hear the monotone sound of the approaching planes. Shortly after, I sighted the first wave of the American B-17 overhead carrying the deadly cargo to their target, the city of Solingen. I observed wave after wave thundering overhead. An hour later, the city joined the hundreds of other cities of devastating destruction. While I observed most of the air attacks at night, this time I had the chance to watch the full impact of the senseless murder of so many innocent civilians.

The destruction was not complete, and on the next day, a Sunday, a second attack destroyed the city. The following news report was announced the next day:

> Everywhere, there was destruction, and almost everything burned again. The fire brigade counted two hundred major fires, four hundred middle fires, and six hundred small fires. One thousand six hundred and nine apartment houses were destroyed. Twenty thousand people became homeless. On November 5, the English radio reported, "Solingen, the heart of the German steel merchandise industry, is a destroyed, dead city."

The propaganda leaflets dropped from the Allied planes could not convince us of the gruesome culpability of the Nazi regime. Anyone that had witnessed the senseless killing of so many women and children by the

Allies found the contents of those leaflets to be absurd. It was for us an unbelievable accusation that was stated in those leaflets—the killing of Jews and other civilians by the Germans—and that at the same time tried to convince the German people of the good intentions of the Allies. Observing the reality we witnessed daily and comparing this with the written propaganda of the Allies, the Nazi propaganda machine had all the aces it needed to convince the German public of the Allies' intentions to finish what was started at the Treaty of Versailles: the destruction of Germany.

Still, there was the doubt of truth. Who was the real foe of the German people? The split of people that were dogmatic to the Nazi doctrine and the doubter was more than ever visible. It was especially evident after the failed assassination of Hitler on July 20, 1944. I remember the day when I stopped at a bicycle shop, and an older lady, over eighty years old, hurled into the shop, weeping and screaming, "They tried to kill our beloved Fuehrer." She started to pray for his health.

Telling jokes about Hitler and his regime was prohibited. Violators faced strict punishment. In spite of all this, a former classmate from the Catholic school and I exchanged the newest jokes about Hitler on our way home from Sunday morning Mass. Itze was the only person I could trust, although he was a leader in the Hitler Youth. He would later save my life.

The brainwashing at school and the Hitler Youth went so far that we were told it was our duty to report anyone that was listening to a foreign radio broadcasting station, even if they were our own parents. Besides all my brothers and sisters, the one that seemed to hate the Nazi regime most was my sister Gertrud. She was staying up late every night, and no one was aware that she was listening to the German language BBC. It was long after the war that she conceded to me what she did.

At one time I remember, I was home alone. When I tuned the dial on our small radio, I heard the speaker in a flawless German language announcing an incredibly unbelievable story. Assuming it was the BBC, I turned the volume to a whisper. The speaker announced, "SS bandits slaughtered in east Prussia ten thousand Jews. Some of them were hanged on streetlights." Scared and in disbelief, I did not tell anyone at first. Later I told my mother what I had heard, but only after I had her assurance she would not talk to anyone about this.

Paul had only been in Russia a short time when we received the message that he was wounded. A Russian bullet penetrated his right arm. After a few weeks at an army hospital, he came home for two weeks on furlough before going back to the Russian front. When he was home, he also visited the factory where I was absolving my apprenticeship. It must have been one of the proudest moments of my life, the way his former coworkers admired my brother. When I walked next to him on our way home, watching his small officer's sword on the side of his sharp uniform, I wished that someday I would make the same impression as my big brother did.

There were many times that I was confused. There were occasions when I liked to be part of the Hitler

Youth, and other times I was revolting. The things I liked at our meetings were scouting and track and field sports. What I hated was sitting around and learning new songs or the marching drills.

The underground organization against the Hitler Youth was an organization named the Edelweiss Pirates. Their distinctive sign was the flower edelweiss. Some days I thought that it would be much more interesting to belong to this organization than to the Hitler Youth. One day I decided to test how far I could irritate my superior. At work, I made myself a belt buckle and decorated the same with a replica of an edelweiss. Then I appeared at our next meeting proudly with my new belt buckle. It could not be worse than if someone had shown up at a synagogue with a swastika. The superior tore off my beautiful masterpiece with the warning that the next time he would report me to the higher authorities.

At the beginning of 1944, I was sent for two weeks to a pre-military ski training camp in Austria, near Innsbruck. I had no idea why I was chosen from all my friends and colleagues. Maybe it was because of my physical abilities as a gymnast. When we arrived at Wattens, at the end of our long train ride, a member of the Hitler Youth greeted us. He led us to a wire rope railway for baggage. He ordered us to place our knapsacks onto the container and sent us—five boys—on our way to the camp located about seven miles away.

It was winter, and it was snowing when we started our long journey up through a snow-covered valley between the mountain ranges toward the destination called *Wattener Lizum*.

After five hours stomping through the high snow, we arrived at the camp. There, members of the mountain troops of the German army greeted us. Although we were only fourteen years of age, they fitted us with uniforms of the German army. We were lodged in barracks, four boys to the room, with simple bunk beds. The food consisted mostly of rice or pasta but was never enough. Every day we had to take a pill against altitude sickness. The pill certainly did not reduce our always-present hunger. The rations were very small. Some boys received food packages from home; one of them was my roommate, a boy from near Vienna. He came from a large farm and received almost daily food packages from home. It was no bother for him sitting on his bed eating the bacon and hams until he could not move anymore. He must have known about our constant hunger but never offered any of the food to us.

Then came the day of locker inspection. The sergeant who made the inspection pulled from the fat boy's locker all the food he had hoarded for so long. Some of the bacon and meat was saturated with maggots, and the bread was moldy. As soon as the inspector was gone, I and the other two roommates started an argument with the fat boy, and it ended with the beating of the chubby boy, who would rather let the food rot than share some with us.

There were also times with great pleasures. For example, we made a cross-county tour with our trainer, who was a gold medal winner at the 1936 Olympics. We stopped our trip at a small block house, romantically located in a snow-covered forest. The old, white-bearded hermit who inhabited the small house demonstrated to us the art of woodcarving. He also showed some of the violins he made. At the end of our visit, he served every one of us with a cup of hot chocolate. Where he acquired the delicious drink from in the middle of the war was a mystery to us.

At the end of our stay at the camp, we loaded those boys that had broken bones from accidents onto sleds and started the long way down the valley to the train station.

My apprenticeship was daily interrupted by alerts of hostile fighter planes. The planes emerged suddenly, and their pilots must have had great pleasure hunting anything down that was moving with their onboard machine guns. During the attack on our city, our trade school was destroyed, and we were assigned to another temporary school at a nearby city. The ride by train to the school was often interrupted by an alert. Everyone had to leave the train and take cover along the tracks. Thank God we were never attacked on our ride. However, I remember an incident. A woman from our vicinity was alone on a country road when suddenly a fighter plane appeared. The woman jumped into the ditch, but it was too late. She was shot in her legs, and one of her legs had to be amputated.

By now, Heidi and I were the only children at home. Maria, four years older than I, was also drafted

into the air defense, and Anita, three years older, was in the German labor force.

Assignment West: Building the Last Defense Line

In summer of 1944, my apprenticeship was interrupted again when I was called to the assignment west. I had to report together with another large group of boys to a small castle near our city where we were briefed about our assignment. From eight siblings, only Heidi remained at home.

We were told that we would leave by train to an undisclosed locality and that we would be away from home no longer than three months. The purpose of our assignment was to build foxholes and construct tank traps and barbed wired barricades to stop the fast-approaching American troops before they could get into Germany. We were requested to report with our Hitler Youth uniforms. I had no problem with that since by now I had finally acquired a brown shirt. The knapsack and a container or a dish for our daily food was also required. I was lucky that my brother John's knapsack was stowed way in our basement. To acquire a dish was more of a task. It was just a few months before the end of the war, and most of the simple necessities of daily life were very scarce. Therefore, I did not have a dish to bring with me at the time I had to report for my duty.

The day of our departure was very emotional. On our march toward the distant train station five miles away, the streets were lined with parents who waved us good-bye. I did not expect my mother among the crying women lining the road; it was, after all, seven miles from our home. It is still very emotional for me remembering the scene when suddenly my mother appeared in the crowd. She spotted me and came as fast as her bandy legs allowed toward me, handing me a brown enamel-coated dish. With a "Take care of you," she disappeared into the crowd while we marched on. I never found out how she obtained the rare utensil. Without it, I would have had to ask one of my comrades to loan me his dish after he had his portion of food.

We left on a large train filled with fourteen- to fifteen-year-old boys. Some young girls from the BDM, the female organization of the Hitler Youth, shared the train ride with us. They had to dish out the food and cook at times when our food supply route was interrupted.

Our first destination was just a few miles from the Holland city of Venlo. The school of the small village was our home for the next few weeks. Our group consisted of about a hundred boys and five girls. The local farmers supplied the straw for our bedding, and the German army dished out two army blankets.

The next day, after receiving shovels and pickaxes, we were led to a nearby field at the outskirts of the village where we were united with all the other groups from the surrounding area. Soon there was a long row of boys as far as we could see.

A few miles away, there was another group of men, fifty and sixty years old, belonging to the newly established Volkstorm. This was similar to a home guard, and it was a last resource of the Nazi government as a bulwark against the enemies. Thinking back, it was more like calm wind instead a storm. Anyone that was too old to join the regular army was drafted into this organization.

In the fall of 1944, they also were ordered to the assignment west. Our first job was to create a tank trap many miles long. After a rough survey and the stake-out were completed, we were divided into small groups. Some of us had to work with a shovel and others with a pickax.

The trench was to be about fifteen feet across, V formed, and fifteen feet deep. To be able to get the soil from the trench floor to the surface, we worked in three stages: from the floor to about the middle of the trench and then to the surface. The workgroup that achieved the most on a given day was rewarded with a weekend off.

During the night, we had to take turns keeping guard at the entrance. Fall was in the air, and the nights were cold and crisp. While standing out there armed with a spade, I wondered sometimes what I would do with my spade if the Holland underground attacked me. I remember that I was freezing cold waiting anxiously for the fifteen-minute intervals of the church bell to ring, counting down the long two hours. I couldn't wait to tuck under my warm blanket on my primitive straw bed after I awakened the next boy to stand guard.

One of the boys was accused of stealing some bread from the small building where the bread was kept during his guard duty. This was the lowest crime a person could commit and was called *Kameraden Diebstahl*, meaning stealing from your comrades. I still see the bloody face of the boy after he was beaten up by a group of select roughnecks.

In the evening, tired from the hard work, we waited for the scanty food, mostly a watery lean soup, to arrive. It was hard for me to comprehend the way some of the boys conducted themselves when they were inhaling their soup instead of eating it just to get in line for the possibility of another serving.

There were days when we did not get any food. Then we were told that the Dutch partisans had blown up our food supply storage. On one of those occasions, after a few days wait for food, a two-wheel, horse-drawn vehicle pulled onto our school grounds. The vehicle was fully loaded with bread. Surrounded by the hungry crowd, the driver of the vehicle was standing on one side of the cart, his feet balancing his body on the large wheel. When he started to unload the bread, he was passing the bread, two at a time, to some helpers to be stored in a small adjacent building. Some of the boys started with the idea to help themselves to an extra loaf from the opposite side of the wagon, carefully watching the driver's motion. As soon the driver turned around to pass out the bread, a hand appeared at the other side and disappeared with the desired goods. When I was watching one boy after the other vanishing through the door and bringing the trophy into their room, I did not want to stay behind. After watching for a while, I too was able to get a hold of the extra bread, brought it to my room, and hid it under my blanket.

It was only a matter of time before the boy in charge noticed the large cavity on the opposite side of the wagon. After he realized what had happened, he started to cry and said if he could not account for the missing bread, severe punishment awaited him on his return. Our superior, who was observing the whole event, ordered us to return the bread at once, so we did.

Although there was never enough to eat, one type of food, tomatoes, was plentiful. It was the main produce of the region. Was it because the farmers did not have enough help to bring in the harvest, or was the fast approach of the Allies the reason for the rotten tomatoes in the fields? Often we went into the fields where we still found plenty of the ripe vegetables. As a substitute for the missing food supplies, the girls at our camp came up with a good-tasting tomato salad. This was okay for a few days, but eating nothing but the salad longer than that made me sick, even thinking about it. There was one other reason that spoiled my appetite.

The tomato salad, prepared in the same oval-sized tin tub, reminded me of the attack on my hometown the year earlier. I remembered the tub filled with all the bloody body parts of the victims from the bombing, and seeing the tub filled with the pulpy red tomatoes created some flashbacks about that night. Even the size of the tub was identical. It also reminded me of my childhood stories, as well as the bread I carried in the tin tub with my mother from the bread factory.

The city of Venlo was only a few miles from our quarters. On weekends, some of us went on excursion trips to the big city. On our way, we picked some of those ripe tomatoes, and we had a real tomato fight. Thereafter, we picked some more and stored them in our shirts. When we arrived downtown, we placed those tomatoes neatly onto the streetcar tracks, equally spaced a few feet apart. The pedestrians were wondering what we were doing but not for long. They received the answer as soon as the next streetcar came by. It was so funny to watch those tomatoes get squashed one after the other and the red substance landing on the faces and clothing of the pedestrians.

We visited some stores on our way home, where, to our surprise, cigars were still available. This was unusual since this was unthinkable in a German city at this stage of the war. The disappointment came when we tried to smoke one of these marvels. It was almost as if someone would light a rag. The only thing they had in common with a cigar was the appearance. Most of the wrapping consisted of brown-colored paper that looked like tobacco. I was very disappointed since I spent all the money I had on those flimflams to send to my dad.

On the way home, we passed a fenced camp of German paratroopers. Standing outside, we started a conversation with some of them and offered them some of our "good cigars" in exchange for some of their bread, but they knew all about our exchange goods. One of the paratroopers showed some compassion and threw a half loaf of bread from his ration over the fence. We expressed our gratitude and went back to our camp, where we equally divided the bread between us.

The tank trap we were digging took form slowly in spite of the daily attacks of the Allied fighter planes. I always spotted the hostile planes first, and therefore, I was selected as the official lookout. With a short bugle, I had to signal to warn for any approaching plane.

On one occasion, I observed a plane high overhead. After I gave the signal and everyone took cover, I lifted my head and noticed two objects falling down, aiming right toward us. They appeared to be two large bombs. We all pressed our faces even deeper into the ground, waiting for the explosion. Seconds passed by, interrupted by the screaming of some of the boys that could not control themselves, while others wanted to act tough and behaved rather foolishly, giggling. Everyone was waiting for the explosion when the two objects hit the ground just a few hundred feet away. When after a minute or so nothing happened, we slowly walked over to the side of the impact. The two "bombs" were nothing but empty fuel tanks dropped from a German airplane.

Constantly there were German fighter planes in the area to protect us from the attack by the Allied planes. On one occasion, we were watching as a German Messerschmitt ME-109 chased a British Spitfire. Suddenly the pursuer was the hunted, and shortly after, the German fighter plane roared just a few feet off the ground. We watched as the plane cut a light pole like a toothpick and then, after making a ground loop, came to rest on its back. With a bullet through his back, the pilot was still alive and transported to the next hospital.

Located about two miles from our quarter was a large German airfield. On one of our free afternoons, some friends and I went there to explore, although it was strictly prohibited to enter the premises of the airfield. When we came unseen to a big building and entered through the gigantic open door, we noticed an airplane at the center of the hall. Under the fuselage was a large bomb. We also noticed the same size bombs in all four corners of the building. We could not resist inspecting the plane from the inside, so all five of us climbed into the plane. It was nice to dream the plane would suddenly take off and we would be able to fly this plane. We touched all the buttons and levels, but there was no reaction. I acted smart since I belonged for a short time to the flying Hitler Youth. Suddenly my peers promoted me as the authority of the airplane by asking me about what the buttons or a certain lever did. Of course, I knew nothing about that plane, especially since it was a Czechoslovakian plane. Nervously, we all watched the large bombs at the four corners of the building as if we were waiting for them to explode at any time.

When one of my friends asked me what a certain lever would do, I answered, "This will turn on the lights." He believed what I told him, pushed the lever, and immediately a loud noise, amplified by the large hall, filled the air. Panicked, everyone stormed to the exit door of the plane. In all the commotion, the boy that was the first to run for the door had his shoe caught in the coarse floor grid. Since pulling on his leg did not help, we finally jumped over him and made it safely to the outside of the plane. So we thought.

Outside a sergeant from the German Luftwaffe accosted us, who played the trick on us by letting the air out of the landing wheel tires that caused the loud, scary noise. While he scolded us for our actions and being on off-limit grounds, our buddy finally jumped out of the plane without his shoe, his shoe still stuck in the gritted floor of the airplane. The sergeant ordered us to herd ahead of his bicycle, drove us like some cattle to the end of the airfield, and gave us the strict advice never to return.

Of course, we did not take his advice seriously, and a few days later, we returned to the airfield since there was so much more to investigate. This time some other boys consorted with us. Since there were not many personnel in the large complex, it was fairly easy to investigate.

Many of the various buildings resembled single-family houses. Every one of those houses had an obstacle to conquer. Three bombs with a weight of fifty kilograms each were jammed inside the doorways of the house. Wires attached to the bombs were leading to the outside ready to be ignited. It was not a deterrent at all for us to go forward with our exploration.

The first priority of our search, of course, was for food. After we went through some of those units, we found one room with some barrels full of D-rations, mainly awful-tasting crackers. One of my friends found a large barrel with a white granular substance, believing that it was sugar. He could not resist putting some in his mouth. As soon as the substance hit his taste buds, he showed his disgust by spitting all around him. It was a detergent.

Up to now, we had operated without being spotted, but this all changed on our way home to our quarter. As we walked along the runway, we noticed that a commando of soldiers, screaming some orders from far away, followed us. Overpowered by fright, we panicked and started to run. Suddenly we heard rifle shots, and at the same time, we realized that they were shooting at us.

Parallel with the runway was a trench that was narrower than our shoulders. It was our last chance to crawl along the trench until we reached a woody area. As soon as we jumped out of the trench, running for the small trees, a hail of bullets hit the trees, but luckily none of us was hurt. Since we did not wear uniforms, we were most likely mistaken for members of the Dutch underground.

One of my friends wore a trench coat, almost white, and as soon we came into our room, he took off his coat and stuck it into the cold potbelly stove. As we just lay on our primitive straw beds, two of the soldiers stormed into the room asking for the man with the white coat. Our leader took our side and told the soldiers that none of us left the camp that day. Disappointed, the soldiers left, and we were safe. After our leader reprimanded us, things returned to normal.

The day came when the local farmers were invited to get anything that was usable out of the airfield buildings. We watched as they loaded their wagons three layers high with office furniture and other estates, almost too much of a task for the skinny horses to pull. We too scoured through the buildings, climbing over the ready-to-explode bombs, hoping to find some food. During our search, I came upon a box containing a small foldable stove. It was not larger than three by four inches. The rest of the box was filled with dime-size tablets, a solid fuel for the small stove. I was happy when I found one more package that contained ten pounds of margarine.

Our search was suddenly interrupted by the sound of a motorbike. As we looked out of the window, we noted two German soldiers. One of the soldiers stayed with the idling bike; the other came running toward the house. As he entered the house and saw us, he screamed at us to leave the grounds immediately. At the same time, he ignited the fuse leading to the bombs in the doorway. As I stormed out of the building, not leaving my treasures behind, the soldier jumped onto the waiting bike and roared down to the next building to repeat the procedure.

We were only about one hundred yards away when a massive explosion blasted the air. Debris rained down all around us. Luckily, not one of us was hurt. We hastily left the area, as the total destruction of the airfield all around us was in full swing. Some of my friends were laughing at me carrying the ten pounds of margarine. They were not laughing anymore when we returned to our quarter.

The first thing I did when we arrived was to take my enamel-coated dish and set up my little stove. After I lighted the fuel tablet, I put some margarine into the dish and fried a slice of my bread. Soon the good smell of the delicious fried bread filled the hallways of the school and lured a group of boys to my mini kitchen. The bread rations we received now daily were not enough to satisfy our hunger, and therefore, we had to find ways to substitute our rations. When I was asked by one of my friends to fry a slice of bread for him, I demanded a slice of bread from him for myself for my service. Soon everyone came, and I gave them the same deal. No one was laughing anymore.

Our project, the many mile-long tank traps, finally came to completion. Would it, as intended, stop the Allies from entering the German fatherland? It seemed that not even our highest leaders believed that our work had any impact. Why then, to the contrary, did they transfer us from the Holland border to inland near the city of Viersen for another project?

Our job at the new location consisted of digging foxholes and the installation of barbed wire traps. The project was to be the new defense line for the slowly withdrawing German troops.

Again, I was ordered to be an observer of hostile planes. On one occasion, I climbed a tall walnut tree nearby to have a better observation point. Killing the time by cracking some of the delicious walnuts, I suddenly noted some fast-approaching planes. After I gave the signal, everyone went for cover. What would be their target this time?

As the planes came closer, only a few hundred feet off the ground, I differentiated that they were American fighter planes. While the planes roared past our position, I could see the faces of the pilots. The planes made a big circle, climbed to a higher altitude, and from there went into a nosedive, activating the machine gun, and released their small bombs into the nearby city. Often the planes were so close, and again I could observe the faces of the pilots.

During all this, I heard the voice of my leader from below giving me the order to come down from the tree immediately, but I answered him, "No, I'm just fine. I can't ask for a better place." Of course, the fat end came when I was back on the ground. The consequence was that my job as an observer was taken away from me, and I was assigned to the main commando station as a messenger.

My job now consisted of delivering messages from one station to the other. The only drawback of this assignment was the long walks. On one of those walks, I passed an orchard with delicious-looking peaches. Finding an opening in the thick surrounding hedge was easy. During the picking of the ripe, delicious fruit I felt a natural urge that could not be disregarded. As soon as I pulled my pants down, I noticed the owner through the branches of the trees walking toward me. I did not wait until my pants were back in place. I just ran toward the opening and forced my way through the small hole. When I felt safe back on the road, I realized that I left my belt at the place of disgrace. Holding my pants up with my hands, I still had a few stops to make delivering the messages.

When I came back to our quarter late in the afternoon, I was ordered to the office of our highest leader. When I was standing at attention in front of him, I felt my pants slowly sliding down. When I tried to grab them, he asked me where my belt was. I said that I lost it. He then walked behind his desk and came back with my belt in his hand. He handed it to me and said with a grin on his face, "Whatever you do, don't get caught the next time." With this, I was dismissed.

My friends told me afterward that during my absence the whole group of about two hundred and fifty boys had to report at the schoolyard. Our leader, accompanied by the man that caught me at the orchard, searched for the boy who belonged to the belt. Of course, no one came forward. I was glad that I was not there.

From the very first day on, I played with the idea just to take off and go back home. I changed my mind and thought about the consequences when I witnessed the following. Our complete outfit had to assemble on the schoolyard. Five boys, led by some of our leaders, were presented in front of the whole assembly. We were informed that those five had tried to escape and now would be punished for treason. We all would witness what would happen to traitors. One of the leaders asked a boy standing close by him to hand over his Hitler Youth knife. I must emphasize that it was strictly prohibited to sharpen those knifes; on the contrary, the edge had to be blunt. While one of the leaders was holding one of the boys, the other started to cut off the boy's hair. Since the knife was not really cutting the hair, they were more ripped out than cut. When they were through with the boys, blood was running down their faces, and they were led away to the basement of the school, where they remained for a full week. What and how much food they received, I do not know. The leader proclaimed, "This is a warning for all of you. Anyone that tries to defect will be treated the same way." After this macabre event, not one of the entire unit deserted. I too decided to stick it out until the end of our assignment.

The long-awaited day came when the foxholes and trenches, surrounded by barb-wired stumble traps, were completed, and at the end of 1944, we were sent back home. It was a depressing moment coming home, where only my father, my mother, and my youngest sisters, Heidi and Franzi, remained. Franzi, who completed her service at the labor force, was now working as a secretary for a small company.

Not too long after I came home, I received a request—as did most of my buddies—to report for a physical. The physical consisted of the typical routine we all had to go through to find out if we were fit to be drafted into the army. I was fifteen years old. We had to wait outside until the last one had his examination. We were then ordered to assemble in a horseshoe form at a nearby plaza. To our surprise, we were greeted by member of the Waffen SS (SS Army). He spoke to us about the glory of the SS and what a great honor it would be to fight for "Fuehrer and Fatherland" in ranks of the SS.

While he spoke, some of us standing at the back rows found it rather comical when we observed his belly dancing up and down every time he screamed in ecstasy his message across the plaza. His lashing words, however, got lost in the wind. Not one of the boys voluntarily joined the "glorious" SS.

My sister Anita was serving in the labor force while my sister Maria was drafted into the antiaircraft defense task force. My oldest sister, Gertrud, completed a study as a nurse at a local hospital. Now she worked as a live-in nurse and house cleaner for a family where the man, an engineer, was bedridden with tuberculosis of the spine. My brothers Paul and Willi remained at the Russian front, where the retreat of the German army was part of the everyday news. How much longer would this horrible war last? Would we ever be united as a family?

Christmas of 1944 was a not a joyous one. The day and night warning sounds of the sirens had no respect for the holiest of all holidays. While we were standing at the manger praying for our loved ones, it was a mockery when we started our traditional song of "Silent Night." Our song was interrupted by the screaming sound of the sirens.

As all the other years during the war, we received at Christmas a special allotment of a few ounces of meat and sugar. We all were looking forward to our Christmas dinner, and this year it was to be a whole pork cutlet for everyone. While we were praying at the manger, the air was filled with the smell of the frying pork chops on the large kitchen stove. As the announcement of approaching hostile planes came through the warning system, we hurried to the basement, our shelter, but not before mother moved the frying pan with the cutlets to the outer surface of the large stove.

Outside we heard the sound of the approaching planes as so many times before. The bursting explosion of the German antiaircraft grenades suddenly overshadowed the sound. We were glad not to be the target for that night. There was not much left to destroy anyway, but our thoughts were with those poor people that would have to perish during this holy night. As we returned from the basement after the sirens sounded an all clear, our anticipation was turned into shock as we came into the smoke-filled room, horrifically observing the black pork chops in the frying pan. Mother tried to scrape off the black crust and served what was left.

In February of the following year, Paul's young wife, who was eighth months pregnant, received a devastating letter from Paul. In his letter, he explained that he was located in East Prussia surrounded by the Russian troops. He expressed his hope that this letter would still get out and that it would still reach us and stated with only a few words that they had only two choices: one, being captured by the Russians, or two, fleeing with one of the refugee ships over the Baltic Sea. Little did we know then that this would be the last living sign we received from Paul. Later we learned that not many refugees escaped the many Russian submarines. They were stationed at all the harbors and sunk every refugee ship, the last hope for thousands of civilians and soldiers. The unknown of my brother's destiny still haunts me to this day.

I think that our mourning over a missing person is not as intense as over person that was killed in action, as this is final. The hope of a missing loved one's return never leaves us, and, while time goes by, the pain of the loss minimizes because time heals. The war could not last much longer, and not many cities escaped the murderous fireworks of the destruction. On February 13 and 14, 1945, the finale with the horrible destruction of the city of Dresden ended. The estimated death toll reached from eighteen to five hundred thousand. The real number will never be known. A few months later, one final destruction of a city took place, whose name would be known by every human being on this earth: Hiroshima. Every future massive detonation would be compared to this atomic explosion and, henceforth, would be a permanent reminder of what our human race was capable of.

Fifteen-year-old Soldiers: Hitler's Last Reserve

At the beginning of 1945, I received an enlisting order. Even though I was only fifteen years old, I was ordered to join the army. Alfred, my best friend, received the same order, and he was even eight months younger than I was. We were ordered to assemble at our Hitler Youth headquarters, and from there, we marched the twenty-mile distance to the small town of Witzhelden. I hoped so much that it wouldn't come to that, that the war would come to an end before I had to go too, and my mother's crying did not help me either. I thought about the prediction my brother John made to my mother at the beginning of the war: "You will still send all your children into this war!" Finally his prediction came true, with the exception of my little sister Heidi, who remained at home.

Our quarter was a large rural barn where we received our army uniforms. At the age of fifteen, I was only five feet, four inches tall. The distribution of the uniforms went by the motto "one size fits all." When I tried on the jacket, my hands were completely hidden by the long sleeves. The shoulder pads were hanging down at my upper arms. The length of the jacket would have suited me nicely as a full-length coat. The real surprise came when I slipped into my pants. While I was pondering what to do with that extra length of leg, I searched and found a few pieces of string at the barn. After I managed to fold the extra length of the pant legs to the inside, I fastened the pants legs with the string around my knees.

The following day, we were taken to a nearby meadow, a clearing in a large forest. One of our high leaders gave us some instruction and then tried to brainwash us about the importance of our service for the final victory for Germany.

My eyes wandered around the other boys. Their appearance was nothing but a joke, and I felt the same about myself. If it had not been so sorrowful, one could even have laughed about it.

After he had finished his speech, he commanded us from our relaxed position to attention. Then came the great moment when he accepted our oaths to give our lives for the "Fuehrer and Fatherland." Now we were finally "real" soldiers, although we did not have any weapons. Little did we know then what our leaders had in mind and how we were supposed to stop the every day closer-moving Allies.

The food supply at the camp was always scarce. Alfred, my best buddy, was lucky since his family was the only family that lived at our house that had a chicken coop with some chickens. Therefore, his mother packaged about ten boiled eggs for him to take on his journey. As we were sitting next to each other on our straw beds, he opened his backpack and pulled out the eggs. While I watched the unveiling of the eggs with mouth-watering expectation, Alfred started to eat the eggs right under my nose without offering even one to me. Too proud to ask him if he would share an egg with me, I turned away, disappointed about the selfish action of my best friend. Not too long after the incident, we were ordered to assemble into a marching order. The destination this time was a town by the name of Hueckeswagen, about twenty-five miles away.

On our way through some small towns, weeping women lined the streets. It had to be a depressing sight for them seeing fifteen-year-old boys dressed in over-sized uniforms and without weapons as part of the last effort to stop the well-equipped American army.

At our arrival at Hueckeswagen, we were quartered in a large school together with about five hundred boys the same age as we were. The rooms at the school were completely empty. There was nothing on the floor to lie on. I searched outside to find something suitable to sleep on.

Thinking that I was lucky when I found an old mattress, I started to carry the mattress up the stairs. I was stricken by an unbearable bad odor coming from the mattress. I was able to throw the stinking mattress outside before I vomited.

The major change at our new quarter was our leadership. While our former leaders came from the ranks of the Hitler Youth, our new leaders were members of the

SS. The disciplinary actions were much stricter now. Fortunately for me, it lasted only a few days.

It came to me as a surprise when I ran into my friend from school, Itze. As I mentioned earlier, he was one of my friends I could trust with my life. I also was surprised when I met him in his new uniform as KE Fuehrer, translating into "war action leader." It was a certain exquisite group of the Hitler Youth equipped with .22 caliber rifles. After we had our normal conversation, I revealed to him in confidence my plan of desertion. He pleaded with me to abandon my plan and told me that they had the strict order to shoot without warning anyone that would try to escape, and since he did not know where he would be posted to help me, it would have been too dangerous for me to go through with my plan. I took his advice and postponed my escape to a later time. It was the last time that I saw him. Itze died two years later at the age of only seventeen years from a rare intestinal illness.

A few days later at around midnight, we were ordered to assemble at the schoolyard, where one of the higher SS officers awaited us. In his speech, he revealed to us that at any given time we would leave the compound and would march eastward to the city of Halle on the river Sale, about three hundred kilometers away, to fight against the Russians. While the exact time of our departure was still a secret, he gave us the following warning: "Any one of you who deserts will be shot by me and thrown into the ditch to rot." Well, if that did not scare me out of those oversized pants, what would?

The sound of a bugle woke us up the same night at about two thirty. After we were summoned again to the schoolyard, we left the inhospitable place and started to march into the early morning.

Our grotesque-looking group of five hundred strong was guarded by two SS soldiers at the front, two on each side, and two of them at the end. One of the soldiers at the end of our group was equipped with a bicycle, and he had to stay with each one of us who had to step out to relieve himself. While we marched for about an hour along the dark country road, I was waiting for the right opportunity to vanish into the night. By now we were only about thirty kilometers from home, and with every step we made, the distance from home increased. I took my chance when I observed that one of my friends had to make a pit stop while the guard that had the bicycle stood with him. With only one other guard nearby, I also asked for permission for a pit stop.

He replied, "You have to wait until the other boy comes back."

"Okay, then I will pee in my pants," I answered with an angry voice.

Then he said, "Go ahead; hurry up, and then come back with the other boy!"

Dangerous Desertion

The road was lined with large trees on both sides. Hiding behind one of those trees alongside the road, I waited until I could hear the stamping sound of the other boy trying to keep up with the SS soldier on his bicycle. Just as they reached the point where I was waiting, a truck came toward us, and when the truck was at the same level as we were, I jumped down the embankment. Since the two were on the opposite side of the road, I was sure that no one noticed my disappearance.

The assurance I gave to myself that I was safe now was weakening by the minute and finally turned into fear. I asked myself, *What if those five hundred boys are ordered to search for me?* I saw myself already being the first victim of our leader, being shot and condemned to rot in the ditch, as he pledged. There was only one way out. I had to crawl out of my hideaway and catch up with the group.

While I was running down the road to catch up with the group, my backpack jumped annoyingly up and down. The string around my knee had become loose, and one of the legs from my pants slipped down over my shoes. While I was trotting along, I suddenly heard my name from behind one of the trees. It was my friend Alfred, who had also managed to get away. The fear of being discovered vanished the instant I saw Alfred. We both decided to run across a field to a nearby farmhouse to hide.

A dog started to bark, and the light in the house, visible through the cracks of the blackout paper that covered the windows, turned on. Haunted by fear of being discovered and turned over to the authorities, we ran until we came to the river Wupper. Here we had only one choice: to cross the deep water. When we finally reached the riverbank on the other side, both of our wet pant legs covered our shoes and hampered us while we walked a short way down the street.

It was dusk when we noticed a horse-pulled wagon coming our way. Impulsively, we hid behind some bushes and let the covered wagon pass by. We saw that the driver was a farmer.

As soon as the wagon went by, we ran after it and jumped into the rear of the wagon, closing the canvas enclosure behind us. Suddenly the farmer turned around to find out what the commotion was. As he became aware of our invasion, he shouted for us to get off his wagon. We pleaded with him to let us stay and said we wanted to go home. We must have made a pathetic impression on him because he suddenly changed his mind. He ordered us to stay, and he would drive us through the town, which was, according to him, crowded with SS soldiers and war action leaders.

We made it finally through the town without an incident, and when we arrived at a forest to the side of the road, the farmer gave us the sign that it was all clear. With a "thank you," we disappeared into the forest and watched as the farmer turned his wagon around and went back toward the town. Sometimes I wondered if our guardian angel appears sometimes as a normal human being, maybe as an ordinary farmer.

Avoiding the main roads, we struggled through the forest, and a few hours later we finally arrived at home. There I found my sister Franzi as the only one present, and she was quite surprised to see me. After the first shock, Franzi told me that my mother was on her way to see me before we were moved out from our quarter that was so close to home.

It was late that night when my mother returned home, saddened that she did not find me. When she saw me, she first could not believe her eyes. I was hoping that she was happy to see me, but instead she started to cry and said with an undertone of accusation, "How could you do a foolish thing such as that? Do you not know that they will kill you if they find you? As much as I am happy to see you, I am equally scared to see you shot or hanging from a lamppost."

I answered, "I am sorry that I acted stupid, and by tomorrow morning, I will leave and try to catch up with my unit." When I talked to Alfred the next day, he said that he would rather like to stay home.

It was very close to the end of the war. Like a distant thunderstorm, the noise of the battlefield was coming closer as the Allies moved toward our hometown. We heard many stories about special units of the German army, the "Flying Tribunal," whose mission it was to find renegades from the German army who tried to escape from combat. With a swift tribunal, they sentenced and executed the death sentence on the spot for those that were captured.

While I was putting on my uniform to leave home the next morning—at least my mother cut my pants to a reasonable length—thoughts came into my mind. *What if I am on my way, honestly trying to catch up with my unit? I am only sixteen and too young to die by the hangman squad.*

As I was parting from my mother, Heidi, and Franzi at our front door, a boy came running down the road announcing, "We are surrounded by the Americans; no one can get out of town anymore."

The imminent approach of the American troops was frightening but also a blessing for me. The fear of being found by the "Flying Tribunal" was over, and I hid my uniform and my backpack in our basement. What could we expect from the Americans? Would the Nazi propaganda turn out to be the truth? Would they kill every man and rape all the women? We knew them only through our experience of the barbarous bombing and what we believed of the printed lies on their leaflets.

The next day troops of the German army moved into our house. None of the soldiers had any idea that we had abandoned our unit, and I think with the war so close to the end, they didn't care and were more concerned with what would happen to themselves. They set up a radio center for all the other nearby units.

Their headquarters was in the laundry room down at the basement. One evening a general came for inspection. The soldiers told us that it was General Model, a highly decorated officer of the German army. The next day he killed himself in a nearby forest.

Trucks with telephone and radio equipment were all around us. Every family had to quarter as many soldiers as possible. We also took in a young soldier whose home was in Bavaria. The little food we had was shared by all of us. When a good friend I knew from school promised to give me a pound of oat flour, I was happy. The only drawback was that I had to pick it up at the other end of the town. He lived about six kilometers away. While the audible rumbling of the battle line moved closer, I started my journey hoping to make it back on time before the Americans arrived. I knew my mother was able to make some kind of dish from the flour since we did not know where we would get our next meal.

Where Are the Rapists and Gangsters?

On my way, I passed an idle German military transport train with no one on board. When I found a case with hand grenades, I put two of the egg-shaped grenades in my pocket. I also found a flare pistol. Since it was too large for my pockets, I hid the pistol under my shirt. It was time to continue on my way home.

Some people on the streets conversed about the Americans that could arrive at any time while many houses showed white sheets as the sign of surrender. When I came to the main street, I noticed a lot of commotion. Here I sighted the first American soldiers. Agilely and very quietly they progressed in one line on each side of the street. With amazement, I watched every one of them. Walking next to them, I tried to keep up with their swift movement. I remembered the front page of the Nazi propaganda magazine, the picture of the black soldier with a knife in his mouth. While some of the soldiers exhibited stony faces, others gave us a smile. Was this the same enemy that so brutally shattered our cities and killed the innumerable women and children?

While I was still puzzled watching the soldiers, I ran into Rudolph, the brother of Kathryn and Andrew. We both then walked next to the Americans down the street. Suddenly I remembered the grenades in my pockets and the flare pistol under my shirt. When I told Rudolph about the deadly weapons I was carrying, it drew the same reaction as if a swarm of killer bees was chasing him. I finally realized my dangerous situation and vanished into a small alley. After I was sure I was not seen by anyone, I hid the grenades in a hedge but had not the willpower to detach myself from the flare pistol. On my return, Rudolph asked me if I got rid of the weapons. I answered, "Yes," and kept the secret of the pistol to myself.

A nearby bunker specially built as a repository to store dry food and tin cans containing shortening was to be opened for the public. The population received only the minimum essentials from ration cards while some of the higher Nazi officials hoarded the food "for emergencies." Somehow Rudolph found out about the release of the food. He had already fetched a few cases with cans of shortening. Then he asked me to help him transport the cases. For my help, I received a quart-size can of shortening from him. Then we went together to the bunker to find out what was still there. Only a pile of noodles was left when we reached the bunker. Everyone around us was priggishly grasping from the floor whatever was left of the noodles. Since I was not prepared for this situation, I had no container to hold some of the noodles. I ran outside, hid the flare pistol, and took my shirt off and created a knot in both sleeves. Now at least I was able to gather some of the much-needed food using my shirt as a holding device.

Joyful to have some food to bring home, I passed the American soldiers, some of them sitting on a doorstep, conversing with residents. On the last stretch, I encountered a group of captured German soldiers flanked by American soldiers. As they came closer, I recognized the young soldier who had stayed with our family for the last few days. He waved, very depressed, when he saw me.

Finally, I reached home. Next to our house, I noticed three large American tanks shooting their guns toward the other side of the valley. Later I found out that my former Hitler Youth leader, who already lost one arm as a soldier, and his father, a higher Nazi official, tried to defend the valley with their machine gun.

As I stepped into our apartment, it was evident that part of the ceiling in a few rooms had collapsed, caused from the firing of the tank's canons. My mother, delighted about the food I rendered to her, started immediately to cook. She mixed some of the noodles with a large spoon of the scarce shortening I had brought home. It was a delicious meal. When I told my mother that I encountered the German soldier who lived at our home, she said, "It was sad when he was captured. We offered him some of Paul's clothing so he could escape, but he said he would rather be captured by the Americans than lose his dignity, and with that, he jumped out of the window right into to the arms of some Americans."

When I was on my way outside, I encountered a tall GI who just came into our hallway and asked me just one word: "MP?" Since the only MP I knew was the German abbreviation for "Machine Pistol," I answered, "No. No, I do not have a machine pistol."

When he asked the next question, "Where are the Fräuleins?" I almost panicked. I remembered the Nazi magazine and saw myself killed with a machine pistol and my sisters raped.

As he stepped into our room, he tried to talk to my mother. She, of course, did not understand what he was saying and offered him some of our meal, but he declined. When two more GIs came into the room and one of them spoke a few words of German, it became clear to me that the word MP meant Military Police. The tall one tried to kiss my sister Franzi on the cheek, but with a smile, she withdrew herself from him. Turning to my mother, she said, "I do not want to make him angry, but do I have to do this?" My mother answered, "No, you do not."

After this little episode, we all sat down for a while and tried to understand each other. The fear of the atrocious behavior by the Allied soldiers as described by the Nazis had disappeared. There was much laughter, and soon the soldiers had to move on.

Some sad things happened during the time I was on my way to get some food, just before the American troops moved in. My playmates helped the German soldiers destroy their weapons. As one of them, a fourteen-year-old boy from our school, hit a rifle against a rock to break the rifle-butt, a bullet, left in the chamber, discharged and entered his stomach. He passed away immediately. His father had died already as a soldier.

Easter of 1945 was pitiful. It was only days until the war finally was over, and everything was in turmoil. I do not recall the exact sequence of what happened next.

At the end of the war, hundreds of thousands of captured soldiers of the German army were transported on to the fields along the Rhine River. There they had to endure the most inhuman treatment and dwelled like a large herd of cows. There were no blankets and no tents, just the bare ground to lie down on rainy and cold nights. The minimum food they received was for many not enough. Many died from hunger and disease. According to references, fifty thousand to one million prisoners starved or died from illnesses. The grasslands of the Rhine River were also temporary homes for many boys of my former unit, only after the GIs degraded them by cutting off their pants, converting them into shorts to let them know they were still little boys. My brother John's brother-in-law also was one of the many soldiers that died of hunger on the Rhine fields. In his diary, he described the daily condition at his camp before he died.

The Heritage of Dangerous Toys

Around our home, the German soldiers left behind trucks equipped with the latest radio equipment, many spools of cable, field telephones, and cases of hand grenades. A special pastime was the collection of handguns. After a few days, I was able to collect a whole arsenal of Lugers, Walter, and Mauser pistols.

Three of my friends and I went deep into the forest to try out the handguns. Andrew brought an additional one, his father's revolver. The ammunition, suitable for the 7.65 Walter pistol, fit also in his father's revolver. It was the first time that I ever had a gun in my hand. Therefore, I had a surprise coming after I made my first shot at a tree. When I tried to pull at the chamber to load another bullet, the pistol went off, and the bullet took a piece out of my shoe, missing my toe by a fraction of an inch. I had no idea that the gun would automatically load itself. Andrew, who triggered his father's revolver already five times, was not able to fire the last bullet in the barrel. After many unsuccessful attempts, we decided to retract the cartridge. When we were unable to free the cartridge, we finally gave up and left the bullet in the turret.

It was about four weeks later when Andrew's brother Rudolph approached me and asked me for his father's revolver. After I climbed to the overhanging of the roof at our outhouse, I took the revolver out of my hiding place and handed the weapon to him

At the same time, I had the need to go into our outdoor enclosure. As I was sitting on the toilet seat, I left the door wide open. Rudolph was standing at the door with the revolver in his hand. He did not know about the bullet that would not fire. Since I knew that nothing could happen with the failed bullet in the chamber, I wanted to show him how brave I was. Stretching out my hand, I said to him, "Give me that revolver, and I will hold it against my head and pull the trigger, and you will see nothing will happen to me."

He said, "Are you sure?" At the same time, he lifted his arm and pulled the trigger. When I heard the loud bang, I realized it was the closest I ever came to dying. My legs started to shake uncontrollably, and I could not imagine a better place to sit but on the john. I was betting my life that the bullet would not fire, and I almost lost the stake of the bet.

Suddenly we had so many toys, harmless and dangerous ones. Every one of us kids had a field telephone, and with it, we could talk to each other over long distances. There was enough cable on large rolls to supply a larger city. The cable also made a great swing by tying it on to a branch of a tall tree at the edge of a steep slope. Swinging about fifty feet over the ground was the closest to flying. On one occasion, we took a German officer's car that was left behind and rolled it down the street to the edge of the deep slope, jumped off just before the edge of the steep hill, and watched the car disappearing, tumbling down into the valley.

The more dangerous game we played was with the hand grenades. We unscrewed the handle with the fuse and then pulled the string on the end of the handle, which produced a light flare at the top of the handle. We lined up about ten of the grenades and, with the help of a nail and a rock, punctured a hole into the grenades. Then we made a little mound from the poured powder and lit it with a match. The effect was exciting when a large, explosive flame shot up. Years later I realized how dangerous our games were. A little spark from the nail could have caused a disaster and killed all of us who surrounded the scene.

In the beginning, curfew was set at seven o'clock at night. When someone told me that a Czech individual was trading handguns for lard, I packed some of my hidden guns into my old school knapsack. Then I went to find the guy at the address that was given to me. My search for him was without success. When I finally gave up, it was close to curfew. I was still a mile from home when I heard the screaming sirens, warning that curfew had started. It was already far past curfew when I had to pass a side road, where I noticed four or five GIs. When they became aware of me, they ordered me to stop. Watching them walking toward me made me tremble. What would happen if they found the guns in my handbag? Panicking, I started to run, but the soldiers pursued and tried to catch up with me. Since I was so much more familiar with the area, the soldiers had no chance and, after a short chase, had given up, and I arrived safely at home.

The villa up on the hill that housed the physically handicapped people was evacuated and was now occupied by U.S. soldiers. When I heard through a friend that the soldiers at the villa traded chocolate, coffee, and cigarettes, I took one of the guns there. This school friend of mine who spoke some English translated as well as he was able. When the soldiers saw the brand new Walter pistol, they all wanted it. I told them through my friend that whoever gave the most for it would get it. One of the soldiers took me aside and told me to come with him. We went from room to room at the villa, and while he showed me the goodies, he asked me every time if that was what I wanted. I said yes until my little handbag was overflowing.

In a cheerful mood, I went home, where my mother received the coffee. With Heidi, my younger sister, I shared the chocolate, and for my father I had the cigarettes. I kept one package for myself, and this was a big mistake I made. Up to that point, I had never smoked, with the exception as a young boy in school, but that could not be considered smoking. Now it was different. I wanted to try it since many of the other boys were doing it. I was surprised that the first time I inhaled it did not make me cough, and with the other boys standing around me, I was proud of myself. Now I was accepted into the secret club of the smokers.

A few days after the war ended, we received a message that one of my brothers was wounded, captured, and transported to an American military hospital at the city of Bad Wildungen. At first, we did not know if it was my brother Paul or brother Willi. With most of the railroad artery still shattered, it was not so easy to travel to a city that was about two hundred kilometers from our hometown. As I watched how much my mother suffered about the unknown, I suggested that I would like to leave to find out more.

With Mother's blessing, a cross on my forehead, I left the next day with my military knapsack and blanket. Since passenger trains were operating very limited, I searched for one of the few coal trains. Those were diverged many times before they arrived at their final destination, and this, of course, was only one of the many drawbacks. Usually the train had a destination slip on the outside of the wagon. At other times, helpful people riding the train gave me the information of the destination.

I was very lucky and made it the first day near the city of Gießen. When we passed a small farmers' village, I decided to jump off the train and find a place to sleep for the night. As soon as I landed unharmed from the moving train, one of my travel friends on the train threw my backpack down. As I walked toward the village, I felt like a coal miner. Seeing the other peoples' faces on the train, I imagined what I looked like. With good luck, I found a place for the night at the first farm

I came to. The farmer directed me to the water pump at the farmyard, where I cleaned myself. Then he allowed me to sleep the night in his barn.

The Plunder of an Army Supply Train

The next morning I left the farm, walked along the railroad tracks, and passed by a very long American military supply train that was standing on one of the tracks. Far in the distance, I observed two individuals who were running from the train and up the hill. When I came closer, I recognized both of them as former German soldiers.

One of them, an officer, asked me, "Did you see any American guard on the train?"

I replied, "No. Are you planning to ransack the train?" Hesitant, he asked me if I would like to be part of it, and I answered, "Sure."

They told me that they escaped from an American POW camp and were on the way home. The officer suggested that he alone would go down the hill and break the seal of the door to find out if there was any food inside. While his army buddy, a sergeant, and I kept fearful watch, the officer broke open the latch of one of the wagons. He grabbed one of the stacked wooden boxes and, with the heavy load, arduously climbed up the steep hill. The sergeant and I took the box, and all three of us bustled to a nearby shrubbery. Fortunately, I had a fork and a spoon that gave us the ability to force open the box.

Anxiously we ripped the boards away until we found about thirty D-rations. We opened one of the small packages that contained four cigarettes, a pack of chewing gum, some crackers, a small can of ham and cheese, and some chocolate. We indulged ourselves with the delicate food, and while the two soldiers smoked one of the cigarettes, they granted me the chocolate. Then we decided to get one more box from the train. After we divided the plunder equally between the three of us, we had to find a way to transport the precious treasure. For me, there was not any problem because everything just fit into my backpack. Fortunately, I had my blanket and offered it to the two soldiers for now so they could hide their portion.

Contentedly we started the long walk along the railroad tracks toward the train station of Gießen. When we arrived and sat down on one of the transportation carts on the end of the platform, we noticed a black GI with his rifle over his shoulder walking toward us. We played a dangerous game as the black guard walked up and down on the platform, and we hid our spoils behind us. We always had to change position, making sure the guard was always passing in front of us while we hid our loot with our bodies. The soldier just glanced at us every time he walked by but did not say anything. After a while, he altered his patrol to the far side of the platform. That gave us a chance to search the area until we found some cardboard boxes to stow the D-ration packages for the two soldiers so they could return my blanket.

Soon the soldiers found a train that would bring them to their hometown. I also found other transportation, and after many detours, I finally arrived at city of Bad Wildungen, where a short search led me to the U.S. military hospital. When I arrived there, I had to confront the two guards standing at the front entrance. They did not have any idea how scared I was when they asked me whom I wanted to see. Would they ask me about the contents of my backpack? If they did, I would be in big trouble. It was almost a miracle when, without further challenge, I finally arrived at my brother Willi's room.

After he recovered from the surprise of seeing me, Willi told me how shrapnel wounded him during his getaway from the Russian front. He wanted to be captured by American troops rather than by the Russians. Knowing Willi's smoking habit, I was not surprised about his complaint of not getting any cigarettes. Therefore, he was overwhelmed as I unpacked my backpack and handed him about sixty cigarettes. In turn, he let me have his lunch, a delicious bean soup. As I finally had to leave, I found out that the next railroad track that was intact was about twenty-five kilometers away. It was six when I left. Since there was still a curfew at eleven, I had to make the long distance within five hours.

The long road toward the city of Korbach seemed like it would never end. Many times I took off my backpack while I was walking, not stopping at all, and ate some of the tasty ration food. As a dessert, I treated myself with chewing gum.

Finally, when I came to a hill overlooking the city at a distance of about three miles, I heard the sirens screaming the beginning of curfew. *Will I reach the city undetected? What will happen if I am caught with the evidence of the robbery of a U.S. military food supply train?* All this went through my mind while I bustled toward the city.

It was about thirty minutes past the beginning of curfew when I arrived. The small city appeared abandoned, and every citizen seemed to comply with the law of the U.S. military government. Finally, I found a school building where I found lodging for the night.

Shortly after the war, large-scale transmigration took place all over Germany, and many schools served as temporary shelters.

In the cot next to mine was a girl about my age. The girl and I talked until late into the night. She wanted to know everything about me, and she told me in turn a lot about herself: how they fled from the Russian soldiers and, with tears in her eyes, about the raping frenzy that included herself and her mother. Suddenly she was overjoyed when, during our talk, I shared some of my chewing gum with her. It was something new to her. She swallowed the gum after the taste was gone. I told her what my mother told me, that the gum would fuse the intestines together, and she believed it until I told her that it was just a joke. An angry voice came from across the large room and told us to shut up. We complied and went to sleep.

The next morning we said good-bye and good luck, and we each went our separate ways.

When I arrived at home, my parents and sisters were happy to see me. I had to tell them all about Willi and his wound and that he would be home soon. The highlight came when I took the coffee from the D-rations out of my knapsack and gave it to my mother. She could hardly wait for the water on the large stove to boil to serve my dad and herself the long-deprived brew. We all were content after I unpacked some cigarettes for my dad and then the rest of my treasure. However, there was the concern about those of our family we had not heard from: Paul, Maria, and Anita.

The Coal Train Adventures

One of my uncles, my father's brother, released from POW camp, came one day for a visit. My aunt and their children had been evacuated during the war to Austria to escape the bombing attacks on our cities. My uncle expressed his concerns about his wife and children. To this day, he had not heard from them and did not know how to contact them. I felt sorry for my uncle and his family, whom I dearly loved. Since I had already some experience of the complicated travel during that time, I offered to search for them. Gratified, my uncle accepted my offer. The next day I packed my knapsack and left for the five hundred-mile journey to Austria.

I was lucky and located a coal train that was southbound for Bavaria. After I climbed up the fully coal-loaded wagon and situated myself onto the black and dusty coal, I met a German soldier who was released from a POW camp and a very attractive young woman. It did not take me long to notice that the two had not just met but had already developed a certain relationship. The soldier called me Bubby, meaning little boy. The soldier, on his way home, was very friendly toward me and took me under his wing like a big brother. After a long ride, it was late in the afternoon, and he proclaimed, "We should get off the train at the next station to find a place to sleep for the night." Before the slow-rolling train reached the station, we jumped off. Wondering where we would find a place to sleep for the night, the soldier said to me, "Your first attempt should always be a church, where logically you will find a priest or pastor who will put you up for a night."

It did not take us too long to find a church where the priest showed us our room to stay for the night. The girl had a small room by herself while the soldier and I were offered the large church hall for the night. After we washed the coal dust off our bodies, the soldier shared some of his food, a piece of bread and a slice of sausage. Then we were ready to hit the primitive cot.

I fell asleep fast but was awakened in the middle of the night by noises coming from the girl's room. When I turned on the light and found the cot of the soldier empty, I had an idea what was going on in the room next door. When I woke up in the morning, the soldier was back on his cot and still asleep. In my innocent mind at the age of sixteen, I always thought that I could see a sign in a person's face that would read: "We had sex last night." To my disappointment, there was no hint in the behavior of the soldier and the girl. Maybe it was just a bad dream.

It was almost noon when the soldier suggested we should first go to the next ration distribution office to get some ration stamps. The release from POW camp entitled him to receive some ration stamps for his travel time to get home by presenting his discharge identification.

My personal identification card, printed on discarded map paper, consisted on the front of fingerprints and the usual information, and on the back was a partial map of a French region. The ID, issued by the Allied military government after the war ended, always had to be carried by every German citizen. While I watched the soldier at the distribution center presenting his discharge identification, he received enough stamps for a period of two weeks. To my surprise, he then said to the person behind the desk, "This young man also needs ration stamps," and turned around toward me, requesting my identification.

With consternation, I looked at the soldier's face and whispered to him, "I can't get any stamps. I get my stamps at home, and I have only my personal identification card." When he insisted, I handed it to him. The person at the counter superficially checked my identity, tore off some of the much-desired stamps, marked the date on my personal identification card, wrote: "Received travel stamps for two weeks," and handed both over to me. The ration was for two ounces of bread a day and four ounces of meat a week. Our next aim was a bakery and then a butcher shop. After we all had a hard roll and a slice of sausage, we had to part. My next aim was the city of Munich.

Before I left, the soldier gave me the advice to replenish my supply when the two weeks passed. Without detection, I played the illegal game of obtaining double rations for a few weeks.

When I finally reached the Austrian border, I found out that there was no way to get across into Austria. Again, I felt that I failed, and this time I let my uncle and aunt down.

After riding in boxcars and coal trains on my way home, I was stranded one night at a freight yard near the city of Giessen. Searching for a place to sleep, I discovered a caboose offside the main tracks. After I got inside the caboose, I took my blanket and stretched out on one of the benches. A feeling of content overcame me before I fell fast asleep. It seemed a few hours later when I was awakened by voices outside the wagon.

As soon as the door opened and a man and a woman entered the darkness of my solitary sanctuary, I made them aware of my presence. Their introduction did not mean much to me, but their friendliness did. It was quite cool that night, and when the woman started to shake, I offered her my blanket. She was very happy about that, stretched down on the bench, and soon was asleep. The man and I talked for a while about the different purposes of our travel. Then he told me that his woman friend was the well-known German writer and sculptor Ruth Schauman. I was not aware who Ruth Schauman was. It was years later when I shared the little episode with my sister Gertrud that she enlightened me about the celebrity Ruth Schauman. Gertrud possessed various books by her.

When I returned home the next day, a surprise was waiting for me. My aunt and her children had already safely returned, and therefore my feelings that I failed diminished quickly.

Paul's wife, Elisabeth, had moved shortly before the war's end to what was later declared as East Germany to escape the daily bombing around our area. During the night of the bombing of our city, the apartment she shared with her older parents was destroyed. She was pregnant and in her eighth month with Paul's child. When Elisabeth asked my sister Franzi to help her through the difficult time of her pregnancy, Franzi left us and went to East Germany. At that time, the American army occupied that particular part of the country. It was shortly after that when Russian troops took over and the border to East Germany closed.

It was early in the morning one day when Maria came home. She brought with her a young individual named Peter she had met on her long way home. We were all so glad to see her, but we also found out soon of Peter's dissimulation. At first, he insinuated that he was in love with Maria, but when he saw a photograph of Franzi, he fell in love with her. I had the feeling that Maria did not care about Peter. Sure, she was glad to have him as a companion on her way home, but now she would be relieved if he just would disappear. He was just hanging around our home, and my mother did not like the idea of feeding another mouth and not knowing where the next meal would come from.

My Sisters Franzi, Heidi, Gertrud, Anita and Maria

When Peter finally suggested that he and I should go get Franzi out of the Russian zone, I was all game. Before we left the next day to the nearest train station to find a train that was going east, my mother handed me a small package. "This is for you; it is all I have," she said. With her thumb, she signed a cross on my forehead, as she always did when one of us left the house. Before we reached the train station, I opened the package. It contained a small cucumber and a small end piece of bread. Peter started to swallow when he saw the meager food. I could not stand it and felt sorry for him, so I shared the food with him.

Finally, after a long wait, a train entered the station. As it moved slowly like a giant snake toward us, we observed those thousands of people already hanging onto the outside, on the buffers, between the wagons, and on the roof. When the train finally came to a stop, all those people started an invasion. They had waited for all these hours on the station platform. Peter and I spotted an empty place on the roof of one of the wagons. With some courageous pushes and pulls, we reached the top, and the train started to move.

It was a beautiful, sunny day, and after a few hours of traveling on the roof, I stretched out. The warm summer wind made me tired, and soon I was firmly asleep. I awakened abruptly by someone grabbing my shirt, and I noticed that it was Peter, who saved me from sliding off the roof.

It was absolute craziness the way some of the other boys and I kept ourselves from boredom during the long trip. Kneeling on the roof, we made bets between us, who came closest with the top of our heads to the swiftly passing overhead constructions and bridges at all the railroad stations. Another pastime was to jump from roof to roof of the speeding train. It probably looked more daring than it really was. I certainly would not repeat this today.

After long hours, we reached the city of Helmstedt, the border city to the Russian occupied zone. We just followed other people toward the border crossing point nearby. After waiting in a long line, the attending Russian border guards refused to let us pass the border. Disappointed, we returned to the railroad station, where a small group of young individuals approached us. They offered to lead us for a fee through the adjoining forest over the border. Since we had no resources to pay them the fee, we had to decline.

It was months later when I read in a magazine about the capture of a serial killer at Helmstedt. Described as one of the individuals hanging around the railroad station, he offered his service to lead people through the forest at the border. He had killed about thirty-five human beings, most of them women. His name was Rudolf Pleil, one of the most notorious serial killers of the twentieth century.

At the station, we waited patiently with hundreds of other people for the next train home. When the train finally arrived, I had the clever idea to jump down the platform, over the tracks, awaiting the train from there. While I was facing the incoming train, I lifted my left foot high enough to be even with the kickboard. Luckily, the train slowed down considerably when I finally set my foot onto the board. At the same time, my body spun around, rolled next to the rails, and in a shock, I watched the deadly rolling wheels passing me by. When I finally recovered from the shock, I got up and entered the train, even finding an empty seat.

The rest of the trip went without any other incident. Peter went on to his hometown, and we never heard from him again. I arrived home the next day. My mother was disappointed that I came without Franzi but was happy to see me unharmed.

For all the smokers, it was a difficult time. We were initially surprised about the behavior of the American soldiers, who smoked only half their cigarettes and discarded the rest. Observing their prodigal behavior, we collected the still burning cigarette stubs, broke the stubs open, took out the tobacco, and when we had a sufficient amount together, we sold the tobacco on the black market.

Suddenly the soldiers changed their behavior. They looked at us adversely and crushed the cigarette stubs into the earth before our eyes. First, we did not understand their behavior, but then we found out that concentration camps with immeasurable atrocities were found. We were at first shocked and later filled with shame. The rest of the world was indignant and shaken.

Shortly after the war, when radio and communication was reconstituted, we heard horrifying stories. Allied troops had found concentration camps where, according to the news, millions of Jews and others were found murdered. Our first reaction was that it was a cover-up for the killings of the millions of German citizens by the Allied air force. It was a few months later, after every German citizen was forced to witness the Nazi perversion and monstrosities at the movie theaters, that we found out the reality. Yes, we noticed, especially during the war, that some of the Jews in our neighborhood disappeared overnight; the explanation was that they were a security risk and were to be deported to a detention camp. They had worked for the Allies and had to be taken into custody for the safety of the fatherland until the war's end. We had no knowledge what happened in those so called "detention camps." It was after the war that we found out about the monstrosities that happened.

The discovery of the concentration camps changed the behavior of the U.S. soldiers toward the German population. The amiability of the first few weeks was now replaced by aversion.

Contrary to the former Nazi propaganda that represented a black soldier as a murderer and rapist, it was especially the black soldiers who were the first tenderhearted toward the children when it came to some food or a chocolate bar. Maybe they could comprehend the feeling of hunger and despair more than anyone else could.

The Beginning of Starvation

We were joyful the war was over, hoping everything would slowly get back to normal. The bombing and the killing had stopped, but the starvation and the lack of daily needs had just begun, and this lasted for another three years. Much was spoken of "care packages" of the U.S.A., but unfortunately, we never got any or knew anyone who received one of these desirable packages.

My friend Alfred and I went to the farm country thirty miles from home. We stopped at every farm and begged for a few potatoes. It was already late in the afternoon, and we had nothing to take home. While we were walking down a country road, we noticed two GI jeeps with a group of soldiers having supper. We stopped and watched as they indulged in the food out of their cans.

We waited patiently like some greedy dogs for their master's leftovers. Since we had not eaten all day, the pain of hunger made us desperate. Finally, the soldiers finished their meals and tossed the cans into the ditch before they left. Expectant, we walked up to the ditch, hoping to find some leftover food in the tossed cans. Looking through the mostly empty containers, I found about a half dozen beans in one of them. The taste of the few beans was so delicious, but the craving for more made me even hungrier.

Every day more soldiers of the former German army released from the POW camps arrived at home. One of them was Albert's brother, Ernst. He told unbelievable stories. He told us about some farmland on the west side of the Rhine River. There, he said, the farmers were glad to give away vegetables and fruits that would otherwise putrefy on the fields.

The next morning Alfred and I left home to check this place out. Midafternoon that day, we arrived at the bridge of Cologne Deutz, the only bridge that was still intact leading over the Rhine River to the city of Cologne. Before we could cross the bridge, we had to stop at an American blockade. They ordered us to get in line with many other people who wanted to also cross the river. When it was our turn, the MP soldier asked us for our identifications and directed us to two other GIs who were equipped with what reminded me of old-fashioned fireplace bellows. They ordered us to lift our arms and blew a white powder all over our bodies. Then we had to loosen our belts, and they blew a large dose on our genitals. The whole episode was to delouse everyone crossing the river. I never had lice, and this was one of the most humiliating moments of my life.

Now we were set free to cross the bridge. During our crossing, we could already see the starved, destroyed city from afar, but the enormity of the destruction came into view when we made our way through the depressing, burned-smelling ruins. War-torn ground always has a certain smell of death. What was once a beautiful city with splendid boulevards and buildings that had survived hundreds of years was now a massive deserted pile of rubble.

We climbed, fatigued, over the dusty rubbish for miles until we finally got to a less-destroyed area. There, even the track of a trolley car was intact. After a short wait, we entered the war-drawn wagon and continued our journey to our destination: a small village between Cologne and Bonn. It was one of the places that, as we were told, was miles and miles of vegetables fields just waiting to be harvested.

We knocked on some farmers' doors and begged for some of the vegetables from the fertile fields surrounding the village, but the answer was always the same: no. Not willing to go home empty-handed, we decided to help ourselves. While Alfred was on the lookout, I went into the field and gathered enough of the lush green for both of us. Gratified that our long trip was still successful, we started our way back to the trolley station.

Apparently, only a few people there were waiting for the next ride to Cologne. At the station, we met a boy and two girls about our age. One of the girls, a pretty blonde girl, got my attention, and I had the feeling that she liked me as well. She started to flirt with me while she was sitting next to me on the trolley.

After a short ride, we all reached Cologne again. Once more, we had to overcome the rubble that led to the rail station. At the station, we found out that no more trains were scheduled for that day, so we did not have any other choice but to camp on the platform. We spread our blankets onto the floor, and I had the privilege lying next to the blonde girl. She started to kiss me. It was the first time that I kissed a girl back. Then she encouraged me to go a step further. I was either too inexperienced or just scared to take the next step, so only the kissing remained. In the morning, we said good-bye and went with separate trains to our respective homes. We never saw each other again.

When I arrived home, my mother appreciated the green vegetables I had gathered; now she did not have to worry for a few days what to cook. Of course, a few potatoes would make it almost perfect.

A few weeks later, I had the idea to ask one of the farmers for a job in exchange for vegetables. He hired me on the spot. The job was hard but worthwhile. My working day began at five o'clock in the morning to clean the cow stables, and after an extensive breakfast, I worked with the farmer in the fields the whole day. The wage was free living in a small room, including the meals and vegetables for our family. If I see a homeless person with a sign today that reads "will work for food," it reminds me on those days.

After six weeks, I had enough of the hard work and went back home.

The desperation to put food on the table was constantly on Mother's mind. I remember when we harvested some rhubarb from our small garden. Mother had the idea; the leaves of the plant should make a delicious vegetable when cooked like other greens. We did not know that the leaves were poisonous. After we ate from the dish, we all turned sick for a few days, but the awful aftertaste stayed with me for months.

The Black Market

It is hardly conceivable today that a bulk of the population covered their daily goods from the black market during the postwar years. After the war, illegal sources often were the only possibility to survive for the procurement of food, like bread and potatoes. Fuel and needed objects like soap and toothpaste were almost unobtainable. The only survival for most people was the famous hamster trip. The word *hamster* is somehow misleading. Generally this means hoarding, but the people that went on those trips to the farmer's countryside were trading some goods, like their tools or china, for some food. Besides acquiring some food through this trade, there was only the black market or theft. Other expressions at that time were "Organisieren," organizing, which meant stealing, or the expression "Kompensieren," compensation, which meant trading. Even many companies went frantically into the compensation to help their employees through those hard times. Our company fabricated beautiful, shiny tobacco boxes, and one machine ran every day to fabricate cigarette holders from aluminum. Those articles were traded in Switzerland for toiletry articles, like soap and skin care. When around Christmas every employee received an assortment of those articles, I picked a cream for my sister Franzi, who was twenty-one years old, as a Christmas gift. I didn't read the description of this cream, and my sister wondered why I gave her a breast increase cream.

Still sixteen years old, I made it my mission to do everything I could to get food for my family. Our area was by now under the British occupation, and the U.S. troops occupied the south of Germany. For the next three years, our situation turned worse, while the people in Bavaria and the south were treated better under the U.S. occupation.

In the summer of 1946, I met a new friend. His name was Paul. He was the son of an old aristocratic family. Little did I know then that we would be friends for life. Paul used to live in the villa we had tried unsuccessfully to save during the bombing. He now lived in an apartment at his uncle's house. His father had a tool-selling business.

When rumors went around that the farmers in Bavaria were ready to trade food for tools and other everyday objects, Paul was willing to supply me with some tools from his father's business.

In the spring of 1946, my friend Heinz and I planned our trip to the area of Würzburg to try our luck by the suburban farmers.

Our first stop was Hagen Westphalia, not far from home. Here we had to find a train to take us to the next stop. After extensive repair of the railroad tracks, more and more passenger trains had started to roll. The train that was going to take us to the next stop was packed with thousands of people on the roof and the footboards. It reminded me of a large colony of bees hanging on to its hive.

At the last minute, when we almost gave up, I discovered a small door on the first wagon. It was a compartment to transport dogs. It was just large enough for the two of us to squeeze in with our trading goods. Once inside it, we were very uncomfortable. We had to take a fetus-like position, Heinz on one side and me across from him. While we were waiting for the train to start, we noticed that the door had no handle on the inside. Of course the dogs that were transported did not need a handle to get out. We carefully leaned the door, not to lock it. Soon the train started to move. Then came the shocking moment when someone on the outside slammed the door shut. The door had at least some slits on the top, which was our assurance to not suffocate.

Sitting there in the crammed position for about two hours, we both felt the urge for relief. We had only two choices: let it just go into our pants or aim at the one-inch draining hole in the floor. We chose the second choice. That did not matter much; we were wet from each other's urine all over anyway.

The train came to a short stop, and we made ourselves known by screaming and knocking on the wall. We heard some noises from inside the wagon, but they did not know where the screaming for help came from, and without any help from the outside, the train started to roll again. It did not take long until we started to worry that we would not be found in time. We imagined that maybe weeks later they would find our skeletons.

We arrived at the point that it was almost unbearable. After about three hours, the train stopped again.

We screamed again for help, and finally it was like a ghost hand opened the door. Heinz and I tried to get out of this hellhole but were not able to stand up and tumbled to the ground. The man who opened the door was standing there in disbelief. It took us a long time to stand up again while we still moved around in our fetal positions.

We had arrived in Bad Nauheim, near Frankfurt. After we picked up our trading valuables, we went into the railway station and stored our belongings at the baggage claim. Here we met another boy who was about the same age as Heinz and I were. The three of us decided to check out the city and find a place for something to drink.

While we were walking down the street and dusk hung over the city, we noticed a bright sign ahead. We decided to go no farther than the sign. As we arrived, it was disappointing. The sign read "Military Police." This was not a place we were looking for. As we turned in to the next street, a jeep with two military policemen came to a screeching stop. The two policemen, their batons in hand, apprehended us and asked for our IDs and then ordered us into their jeep and drove just around the corner. They ordered us to walk with them to the military police office. Here they pushed toward a desk with some officers. Since we were not familiar with the English language, we had no idea what they were saying. The only word I picked out was *prison*.

The boy who was with us was free to go. Heinz and I were scared as they ordered us into the waiting jeep. After a wild ride through Bad Nauheim, we suddenly stopped at a big building surrounded by a high brick wall. Next to the large gate was a sign that read "Civil Prison." After the ring of a doorbell, a heavy-set, older woman opened the gate. One of the police officers pushed us through the gate, and now we were at the mercy of that old woman after she closed the gate again.

She led us into the building and up the staircase. The woman was breathing hard as she climbed up the stairs as if she had asthma or another breathing disorder. Maybe it was her age combined with her weight. While we climbed the never-ending stairs, we asked the woman why we were in such a predicament. She just answered, "You have to ask the Americans." Of course, that was impossible.

On the third floor, she opened a cell door, told us to get in, and closed and locked the heavy door behind her. Heinz and I stretched out on the bunk bed and covered ourselves with the supplied blanket. During all this, we asked each other what we did to deserve all this. We knew we had not committed anything unlawful. The answers we should get the next morning.

We were woken by a hard knock on the door and a voice yelling, "Get up! They are waiting for you!" While we slipped on our shoes—we still had our clothes on—we were hoping that it was all a mistake and that we would be set free. Running down the stairs, we reached the front door of the building. Just as we crossed the courtyard, two German shepherd dogs came running toward us, and there was a loud voice hollering, "Not so fast! Just join the others!"

As we turned around, we observed a group of prisoners walking in a circle. We did as ordered, and I tried to start a conversation with a person that was walking behind me. The person, maybe about twenty years old, told me to shut up and that I should wait until we were around the corner and the guard could not see us because talking was strictly forbidden.

When we were sure not to be seen, he asked why we were there. I told him what had happened to us last night. We had to wait for the next time we came to the corner that could not be seen by the guard to continue our conversation. Next he asked me where we were from and how old we were. I told him that we were seventeen years old and that we lived in the English zone. Next he asked me if we had a curfew in the English zone. I told him no. Then he said, "Don't you know that we here in the American zone have a curfew for youth under eighteen years old not to be on the street after dark?" That explained everything.

When I told him that we had not eaten for almost two days, he assured us that he would take care of that since he was working in the prison kitchen. We prepared ourselves to stay for a while in this place when we found out that one person in another cell was in prison for six weeks already because he sold a package of American cigarettes on the black market.

At lunch, we received our first meal: rutabagas with a slice of sausage and a pudding for dessert. Wow, what a meal. Heinz and I were glad to be in prison for a few days; at least we had food. After three days, two soldiers of the military police picked us up and released us at the front gate, but not before we paid three marks and fifty cents for food and lodging.

We retrieved our belongings from the baggage claim and continued our adventurous trip to Würzburg. We arrived in the countryside, went from one village to the next, and haggled with the farmers the tools for food. Not discouraged by some of the farmers who just showed us the door, we still managed to find some farmers who were ready to trade. We found some farmers who let us sleep in their hay barn. After a few days, I could account for about ten pounds of flour, quite a few eggs, and about one pound of bacon. We buried the eggs carefully into the flour and started our way home. I already imagined the happy face of my mother on my return with all those goodies.

After my return, I was rewarded with a tasty pancake made from the flour and eggs I brought home. To our dismay, the bacon was loaded with maggots. Carefully my mother removed all those unpleasant creatures, fried, and stored the bacon for further use.

The black market was by now in full bloom. The going price for one American cigarette was ten marks, and a half-pound of butter was about two hundred marks. My hourly wage at that time was about eighty-seven cents. This certainly would not go far on the black market.

I had the idea to take a trip to the area of Bruchsal near the black forest. This was an area where tobacco farmers grew the much-wanted crop. If I could get enough tobacco leaves, I would cut it, package it, and sell it on the black market. The money I would get I would use to buy tools and finance my food trips. My sister Gertrud, who was old enough to receive a ration card for forty cigarettes a month, helped me finance my trip to Bruchsal by selling the cigarettes on the black market.

When I arrived in one of the tobacco-growing villages and found a place to sleep for that night, I made the acquaintance of a young man from Holland. He trusted me with his plan by revealing to me that he brought with him one hundred pairs of wooden shoes. He was sure that this was one article the farmers desperately needed. He asked me for my help and promised me two pounds of tobacco.

One morning we set up shop in the middle of the village by organizing a large hay wagon. I helped him load all those wooden shoes next to the wagon. The word was spreading around that it would cost two pounds of tobacco for one pair of shoes. It was not too long until the farmers lined up.

We had a board set up where I had to place the wooden shoes. The "dealer" then gave out the shoes, took the two pounds of tobacco leaves, and threw it onto the wagon. It did not take long, and we collected two hundred pounds of tobacco. Now this was a black market big time.

One pound alone, packaged in fifty-gram packages, would yield about five hundred marks. I was just wondering how he would manage to get the load home. He obviously figured that out already. He came up with some large bedspreads, and we started to load the tobacco into the bedding. We closed it all up safely and attached large signs that read "Refugee goods." He handed me the two pounds for helping. I wished him good luck and good-bye and returned home. I have no idea if he made it safely back to Holland. I was just happy that I got my tobacco.

I was planning my next trip with my friend Paul and his brother Robert. After I sold some of the tobacco on the black market, I had enough money to buy some tools from Paul's dad. Since my last trip to Würzburg was successful, we made this our next objective. We arrived late at a little town called Oxenfurt and immediately went out into the farmers' country. Searching without success for a place to sleep for that night, we noticed a large straw pile in the middle of a field. The decision was clear that this had to do for the night. After we stowed our heavy suitcases full of tools, we all crawled into the pile and went to sleep.

The next morning when we got up, we looked at each other and started laughing. We looked like a bunch of scarecrows. After we cleaned ourselves as much as possible, we took our heavy suitcases and walked toward the road.

The next thing we noticed was a police officer on a motorbike waiting for us. Acting very serious, he asked about our intentions and where we came from.

The straw that was still sticking to our clothes probably did not make the best impression on him. He ordered us to open our suitcases. When he saw our tools, he gave us a lecture that the trading of merchandise for food was strictly forbidden. He ordered us to close our suitcases and follow him to his office, which was about five kilometers away. It was almost unbearable to carry those heavy tools while he was sitting comfortably on his bike.

Finally, we reached his office. He took a seat in front of his old-fashioned typewriter and started to write a police report. We noticed right away that he was not very familiar with a typewriter. Robert, a good typist, told him to move over to show him how it was done, and then he wrote our own police report. After we unloaded all the tools in his office, he told us that we were free to go. With a mixture of sadness and anger, we left with our empty suitcases and started on our way home, where our families greeted us with great disappointment.

It was summer when my friend Paul and I went almost every day down to the valley for a swim. There, we always met some other boys we knew from our school. Often, a very pretty woman, approximately thirty years old, joined us. She would lie in the grassy meadow in a two-piece bathing suit next to the small pond, watching us. Word went around that this young woman initiated some of the young lads into the sexual love life, and those boys were always envied by the rest of us. Little did we know then that this young woman, whose husband was killed during the war, fell victim to a disastrous event.

It began when my friend Alfred and I visited a soccer stage. Before the beginning of the game, we walked around the soccer field. During our walk, we noticed a few children playing on a scrap metal mound piled up away from the game field. We just passed that scene when a large explosion made us swing around, and we saw two of the playing children thrown into the air. We immediately ran to the place of the explosion. There lay two boys, maybe eight or nine years old. In shock, they stared apathetically at their shattered feet, the bloody bones mingled with scraps of their shoes. An undetected mine in the scrap metal pile had caused the explosion. We turned away from the horrifying scene. Later we found out that the mother of the two children was the young woman whom we so often found at our swimming pond.

Growing Our Own Tobacco

My dad and I started to grow our own tobacco in our small plot next to our house. I cannot remember where we got the seeds from, but it was just for a few plants. After a few weeks, we had harvest time. We picked some of healthy-looking leaves and cut them into fine-cut strings. Since we could not wait to have the tobacco dry naturally, we spread them out on a cookie sheet and dried them in our stove for about twenty minutes.

While I had some friends at my home, they all were curious about our achievement as my dad stuffed his pipe for the first puff. Since he seemed to be appeased by the taste, it was now our turn to taste and inhale our new product. Since we had no cigarette paper to roll a cigarette, some newspaper had to do. The problem was that the newspaper was so thick that it would compare with our shopping bags of today. When we smoked those cigarettes, the paper did not turn into normal ashes; halfway through we had to break the black, burned paper off since it would not fall off like cigarette paper.

Then came the day when a friend got a hold of a copy of the *London Times*. This fixed the dilemma of the absent cigarette paper. This paper was so thin that it burned almost like cigarette paper. The news came out that everyone who smoked this weird composition would die within five years.

Shortly before Christmas in 1947, I went to the Bavarian forest, an undiscovered area by "hamsters" and about five hundred miles from my hometown. This time my friend Bubbes accompanied me. After a short train ride from Passau, we reached a little village. A friendly farmer let us sleep in one of his farmhands' beds. While we were walking from village to village, the weather turned bad. It was late in the afternoon when it got so foggy that we got lost. After we noticed that we were walking in a circle, we were scared.

When we finally came to a farmhouse, the farmer showed high interest in the kitchen clock I had in my suitcase and offered me a live goose for it. I thought this was insane. *How can I take a live goose on a five hundred-mile journey?* Then I thought, *How great it will be if I would bring a goose home for our Christmas dinner.* I asked the farmer for a burlap sack and then stuck the protesting goose into it. During our conversation, the farmer asked me if I could get him a drill press and he would trade it for a live pig. I promised to do my best. Back in my mind, I thought, *How will I get a live pig home?*

The next day, suitcase in my hand and the burlap sack over my shoulder, we started our way home. Without any problems, we made it to Würzburg. There were of course many questions from the other travelers, who wanted to know what I had in that burlap sack.

The train station of Würzburg was totally destroyed from the bombings. Bubbes and I decided to leave the station and find something to drink, but what about the goose? When we found a burned-out telephone booth on one of the platforms that was almost half full of ashes and junk, we laid the burlap sack with the goose down into the booth. We were sure that it would be safe there since not a soul was around when we left the station.

On our return about an hour later, we saw, horrified, that the burlap sack was walking and tumbling over the platform. Somehow the goose made it out of the booth and wanted to go for a stroll. Since the sack was well tied up, she could not escape her confinement, and her excursion was restricted. It was therefore easy to pick up my valuable load, and we continued our trip home.

At home, we were expected with anticipation, but nobody could figure out what was in my sack. Finally, we had our goose at Christmas, the first one in our lives, and we felt so rich then.

Sunday, June 20, 1948: Monetary Reform

The economics and the implementation of the Marshall plan required a currency reform. This was first planned only for the occupation zones of the Americans. Up to this day the currency was still called "Reichsmark" and was very unstable. It had almost no value, except on the black market. The wages were in no comparison to those price hikes of the black market. My wage at that time was a skimpy one mark and forty cents.

We all were waiting for this day. Every citizen received forty Deutsche marks. Savings in "Reichsmark," if you had any, were exchanged. If you had one hundred marks of the old currency, you received ten marks of the new one. It was, therefore, practically a new beginning with the new forty D-marks.

The next day, a Monday, all the stores were loaded with merchandise, and the black market disappeared. My friend Egon invited me to come along with him to the city. With his new money, Egon bought a pickled herring and a cigar for each of us. Ludicrously standing in the center of the ruined city, enjoying the herring in one hand and the cigar in the other, we watched as people spent the first D-marks on things they had missed for so long.

The situation slowly turned to normal—whatever normal meant for us. I had not lived a normal life since

I was born. For the first time, all my friends and I could do what seventeen- and eighteen-year-olds did. On Saturday or Sundays, we went to the dance hall, every week to a different one, depending on the quality and beauty of the girls. When we were acquainted with a girl we liked, it was, of course, our duty as gentlemen to offer to bring her home safely. The surprise came when the girl told us where she lived, and it was sometimes eight to ten miles from our home and was, therefore, no surprise that we came home when it was already daylight. There were no cars, no buses, and no streetcars at night we could use on our long journey.

On one summer day, I was on my way home from work in a streetcar. I noticed this beautiful girl just three feet away from me. I could not take my eyes off her. She was about sixteen years old with long, blonde hair and a face so beautiful as I never saw one before. She was looking at me; that was a good sign. It took a few fares with the streetcar until I had the guts to talk to her. I thought, *What the heck? If I lose, so be it.*

After a short conversation, I asked her for a date to a movie. I was so surprised when she said she would be delighted. Her name was Brunhilde. It was the first time in my life that I thought I was deeply in love, and I was seventeen. On our way home from the movie, she unveiled to me that her mother, who lost her husband during the war, was marrying a restaurant owner. She would have to move to another city about 150 kilometers away. I was so sad that day because I thought I found the love of my life and our relationship would end even before it began. She promised me that she would stay in contact with me.

We wrote letters to each other, and in one of the letters she told me that she was visiting her grandmother in our town and she would like to see me. I was so nervous when she invited me for a date. We went to a dance hall, and we had a great day. On our way home, we agreed to meet the next day. When we arrived at her grandmother's house that night, I was not sure how to say good night to her. Very politely, I asked her if she would mind if I kissed her.

She answered, "We have plenty of time the next time." I accepted her answer, and we went our separate way home. I was in seventh heaven and hardly could wait for the next day.

At that time, I was working as a tool and die maker at Egon's father's factory, which was located across from my home at the old school. Next to the factory was a small garden. When I left work the next day, I saw to my surprise Brunhilde working with her mother in her grandmother's garden. We exchanged a few words and agreed to meet that evening. I went home to clean up for my date with Brunhilde. She did not know where I lived, so I think she was surprised when she saw me walking into the old school.

I was excited that evening, and I made sure I was on time at our meeting place. It was an enormous disappointment for me when I waited for about a half hour and Brunhilde did not show up. There was only one explanation: she found out that my home was at the old school.

After the disappointment, my friends and I hit the dance floors on the weekends. On one of these occasions, I met a girl named Sigried. We dated for about six months. With her, I experienced my first intimate love life. At first I liked her a lot; after a while I even fell in love with her. I never met anyone that cherished the color green so much; as a matter of fact, I never saw her dressed in a different color. But the green with her blonde hair suited her well. She was the first girl that invited me to her home and introduced me to her parents. We usually met twice a week in her hometown, Wuppertal. My friend Egon, who dated her girlfriend, accompanied me most of the time, and it took us about an hour and a half ride with the streetcar to get there.

The Beginning of the Rest of My Life

Then came the Saturday on the dance floor that would change my life forever. My friend Alfred, who had no girlfriend that day, accompanied Sigried and me. During a dance with Sigried, my eyes were drawn to this beautiful girl. She was sitting at a table accompanied by a middle-aged couple. She noticed that I was looking at her, and with great encouragement, she looked back at me. I assured myself that I had to make contact with this girl. I had to talk to Alfred. Since he had no girlfriend, I asked him to dance with the girl, who fascinated me. Alfred agreed, and after a few dances, the girl agreed to meet him the next day at the movie theater. She had no idea that Sigried and I would show up.

When we arrived, Alfred was standing with the girl in front of the theater and did not notice our arrival. As the girl turned around, I introduced myself. She was so surprised and stuttered, "Thank you." Then she said, "My name is Marga." Later I found out that she only agreed to date Alfred at the movie theater because she was hoping that somehow she would see me again. The next day Alfred told me that Marga did not want to see him anymore. He was very disappointed, and so was I. He did not know her last name and where she lived. The only clue: she told him that she was in swimming club.

There was only one club in her little town. The next week I went to the club and hoped that I would see her there; even so, I did not like swimming very much. I was more into diving, which was more my style because of my gymnastics skill. I noticed that there were only young males present. Where were the girls? I asked a guy next to my shower. "The girls," he said, "have a different day, and we never train together." *What a bummer*, I thought.

It seemed there was no way to find Marga again. She was not at the weekend dance, and I did not know where to start. Because of her, I revoked my relationship with Sigried.

It was months later and a hot summer day. That night I was planning to see a girl I had liked a lot for a long time. By that time, I had put Marga out of my mind. Before the date that evening, I went to the public swimming pool. I showed off a few jumps and somersaults from a five- and ten-meter diving platform. After a few jumps, I rested on the meadow surrounding the swimming pool. While I watched the crowd, I noticed a girl approaching. I could not believe it; it was Marga. It was like a phantasmagoria. She seemed as happy to see me as I was to see her.

She said that she had been watching my jumps from the platform earlier and was quite impressed. She especially liked the eagle jump I made from ten

The Eagle Jump

meters. My brain seemed to collide with my feelings. I had to make a decision about the girl I promised to date that night and Marga, whom I finally found. At first, I decided on the date and lied to Marga that it was my mother's birthday and I had to leave. Her comment was that it would not be nice to miss my mother's birthday.

The time that I had to leave moved closer. Suddenly I made the most important decision in my life. It is amazing how a split-second decision often influences the fate of our whole lives. I told Marga that my mother would forgive me if I would not show up on her birthday. At first, she insisted that I should go. How could I tell her that it was a lie?

I accompanied her to the nearby streetcar, and we promised each other not to get lost again. Our date was set for the next day, and from then on, we went steady.

I was shocked when Marga told me about the horrible experience she had in her young life. At the bombing of her hometown, Wuppertal, in 1943, she lost her mother, sister, and brother. She was only twelve years old on that horrible night and escaped merely because she was in a different part of the city, where she was babysitting for the children of a woman whose husband was in the military. She also told me that as she was in the basement with the three small children during the air raid, a water main broke and the basement was flooded, and she fought to save the children from drowning. She now lived with her foster parents. Her foster mother was a friend of her mother's.

Engaged

We had a great time together until disaster struck shortly before our engagement. Marga had a terrible hemorrhage, and she was diagnosed as having ovarian cancer. She was only nineteen years old. We were told that she would have only a 10 percent chance of ever getting pregnant and having children, if she even would make it through. She needed immediate surgery and radiation treatment. Six months later, the cancer was back, and Marga needed another surgery. Before her illness, she was dreaming of having six children. I never agreed on so many since I came from a family of eleven children.

Not long after her illness, we were engaged. We spent our last money on our engagement rings. The price was twenty-seven marks each, which amounted to about seven U.S. dollars. The engraving had to wait until our next paycheck and came to three marks each. We were planning to get married a year later when Marga turned twenty-one. Since she did not have a real home, we thought it was the best thing to do.

The Last Prank

Still hanging around with my childhood friends in the evening, there was one last prank to play. The question always was, "What are we going to do tonight?" Somebody had the splendid idea to construct a life-size dummy. We went right into action, and Marga helped us to find some old clothing to dress the dummy. After a while, it turned out very lifelike. The next question was what to do with it. Again, one of my friends had the idea to hang him on a telephone pole, and we all thought it was a great idea and went to work. It looked so real hanging there in the dark of the night that my aunt, who lived close by and was on her way home, saw the dummy and ran screaming down the road toward her home.

We had to agree with Robert, Paul's brother, who by now had joined us and said that this was a stupid idea. He said that an older person could have a heart attack seeing the dummy hanging on the post. Then he said, "Why don't you hang him from the bridge in Müngsten?" It was same bridge I was dangling from years earlier.

We all agreed, and Robert, who was the only one that owned a car, volunteered to drive us with the dummy to the bridge eight miles away. The car was very crowded with the seven of us and the dummy lying across. We arrived at our destination around midnight. After a short walk and singing on the way, we finally reached the bridge. Now the question was who would volunteer to be so stupid and able to climb the 360-foot bridge in the middle of the night with a dummy in tow. The election fell on my friend Bubbes and me.

Against my promise to Marga that I would not climb the bridge, we went on our way. With the thirty feet long cable, a remnant from the German army and the dummy in tow, we managed the arduous climb up the bridge.

I have never been uncomfortable at heights, but this was horrifying. Observing the light sky with all the stars above and total blackness below, it was almost like staring into an abyss. After we reached the top of the bow, we tightened the cable, lowered the dummy down the thirty feet, and climbed the tedious way down. Satisfied with our accomplishment, we all went home.

The next day was a holiday, the ascension of Christ. On those days, many visitors came to the bridge to view the technical marvel. The bridge was the highest railroad bridge in Germany. It was built up from both sides of the valley, and met exactly in the center.

My friend Paul and I made the way to the bridge early in the morning to see how the dummy looked hanging from the bridge. To our surprise, the dummy was gone. We started a conversation with one of the souvenir stand workers that surrounded the bridge. They told us that the police and fire department were there in the morning because they thought somebody hung himself and cut the dummy off. The next day, a note in the newspaper asked for the punishment of the culprits, but no one ever found out.

The Start of a New Life for Two

Our financial situation still was very lean since I handed over my wages to my mother until approximately four weeks before our wedding. Until then, I received five marks as pocket money per week.

Our wedding was in September of that year; it was 1951. The reception was very small; we just invited the closest relatives. We purchased Marga's wedding dress from my sister Franzi, who had married the year before. Since there was not enough money for a veil, a friend of mine offered to lend us his wife's veil. They had married just a few months earlier.

Our Wedding, 1951

Marga, my mother, and some of my sisters did the cooking and baking, and after we removed the furniture from our biggest room, we had enough room for tables and chairs to seat about thirty people. A friend loaned me a record player with some records. It was modern for those times. It had a crank to wind it up and some needles to change when one got dull. Nevertheless, we had music to dance.

Shortly after the war, and with many of the buildings destroyed, it was almost impossible to get an apartment. Since some of my siblings were married and had moved out, my parents let us have one of their rooms. We were able to purchase some furniture, and Marga and I were very happy in our cozy new home.

Marga's foster parents lived in a townhouse outside Marga's hometown. About two years later, when Marga visited them, the next-door neighbor, an elderly woman, told her that we could rent her townhouse. This was the best news we could get. Not long after, we were happy to move into our new home, which needed quite a bit of renovation.

After we lived there for about six years, the woman passed away, and we had the opportunity to purchase the townhouse. Getting a mortgage at that time was almost impossible. The woman's brother, who inherited the house and was just using his sister, requested that we come up with the money within three days or we had to move out. We admittedly possessed the first purchase right, and he saw his obligation with the three-day full-payment request fulfilled.

We were completely dejected since we had put so much laborious work into the house. We did not believe that it was possible for us to raise the necessary sum in this short time. Nevertheless, in the end, we did what we thought was impossible. We made it by taking a loan off my life insurance and other short bonds. Now we were proud homeowners.

Another big help that brought us closer to own our home was a colleague of mine, approximately seventy years old and still working, who knew of our situation. One day he took me to the side and put eight hundred marks into my pocket. He asked only that I tell no one about it and said that I could pay him back whenever I was able to. I was surprised about his trust toward me for a long time after. Of course, he was the first to whom we paid the money back. Marga was as surprised as I about the trust of this old man, but we both were thankful that we came a step closer to own our new home. Marga and I talked about this trusting man for many years and wondered if this episode could still happen today, when so much distrust exists.

Not Again

Then came August 1961, the erection of the Berlin Wall. We had just recovered from the aftermath of World War II, and we were scared that it would all start over again. Marga and I played with the idea to leave Germany and immigrate to the United States to my sister Maria, who was married to a former GI. Shortly thereafter, we put our idea into action. After we sold our home, we left Germany in April 1962. The worst was parting with my old parents and my siblings we had to leave behind.

Arriving in the United States in the state of Michigan, I was planning a two-week vacation and getting used to the new language. With my sister Maria in tow, I applied for a job at General Motors. To my surprise, they called me two days after the interview, and I was hired as a tool and die maker, my original trade.

The first eight weeks were the hardest in my life since my knowledge of the English language was almost nonexistent. At times when I did not understand a person's question and he repeated the question, he did this with the raising of his voice. Then I had to explain that my hearing was okay; could he please just speak a little slower?

There were other language confusions. When Marga and I were on a trip, we came by a sign that read "Ice." Since ice in German means ice cream, I asked Marga if she would like to have some. I went into the store and ask for two ice. When the person came back from the storage room, he banged two bags of ice on the counter. I had a hard time trying to convince the person that this was not what I wanted, so I handed Marga the two bags of ice. We laughed about that long after. It astonished me when I noticed that people were smoking at the supermarket and discarded their cigarette buds in the store aisle. It was remarkable that people were friendlier than in Germany. After eight weeks, I did okay, and I got used to the new language. It was not long after that I was employed at a research and developing department as a manufacturing engineer based on my technical education and my method engineering degree from Germany.

In May of 1967, my father died in Germany at the age of eighty years. Marga and I arrived in Germany shortly before his death. A half hour before he closed his eyes forever, he awoke out of a coma and recognized Marga and me. He was looking at us, and he made the following appeal: "Please take care of that little girl for me!" He then fell back into a coma and died thirty minutes later.

At first we did not understand the meaning of what he had said since we had no children and probably never would have since Marga had cancer at the age of nineteen. It was her greatest desire to have her own family and children.

At work I had a good friend from Switzerland. One day he decided to move to the state of Washington. He wrote me from there and told me how beautiful it was and raved about the breathtaking view of the mountain range. This made me curious since I was not attracted to the flat scenery of Michigan. Shortly after our return from my father's funeral, I asked Marga her feelings about a move from Michigan to Seattle. Marga agreed. I found employment as tool engineer at the Boeing Aircraft Company.

Our Life Is Complete

During our stay in Germany for my father's funeral, Marga's foster parents decided to leave Germany to join us in the U.S. Marga's foster father was a great dog trainer and suggested they move with us to Seattle and start a business training German Shepherds. After their arrival in Michigan, including two German Shepherds Marga's foster parents brought from Germany, we all started our beautiful journey from Michigan through the scenic countryside of the western United States to Seattle. Shortly after our arrival, we visited a German shepherd kennel I had picked out from the phonebook. There we met a beautiful family near Seattle who had already five adopted children besides four of their own.

When Marga fell in love with their newly adopted baby, the woman asked why we did not adopt a child. We told her that we weren't able to adopt until we were U.S. citizens and the ability to apply for citizenship was still a year away. She assured us that her attorney would help us. Through the help of this woman, we were able to apply for an adoption of a child that was only one week away from birth. A little girl arrived a week later, and we had a court appointment two days thereafter. With great anticipation, we arrived with our attorney at the Seattle courthouse that Friday afternoon. After some arguments about our citizenship by the judge, he finally granted us permission for the adoption process. There was, however, the stipulation that we were not allowed to leave the state of Washington with the baby until we were citizens of the United States. This decision threw a curve ball into our preparation for returning to Michigan, where we still owned our house and General Motors had offered me reemployment. After I explained this to our attorney, he had a discussion with the judge. After what seemed like an eternity, the judge finally gave us the permission to return to Michigan, with the stipulation that we would apply for citizenship as soon as we were eligible.

Thanks to the swift action of the court and the woman's lawyer, we were blessed to accept our daughter at the hospital on her second day of life. This all did not sit well with Marga's foster parents. It even created some anger over our "selfishness." The result was that Marga's foster parents returned to Germany and we had no more contact with them.

Now finally our wish came true, and we had our little girl.

We named her Inge, after Marga's little sister who was killed during the war. Was this my dying father's premonition? Shortly after Inge's birth, we moved back to Michigan since the Boeing Company got into an economic chaos and released approximately thirty

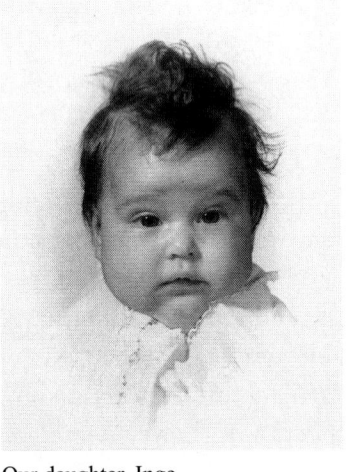

Our daughter, Inge

thousand coworkers. Admittedly, I was not under the releases; however, it was a risk I could not take since I now had a bigger responsibility. I gave notice to Boeing to leave my employment as an engineer. With an increase of my salary General Motors rehired me.

Our daughter, Inge, grew up to be the most beautiful girl in character, looks, and talent. As soon as she could understand, we told her that she was special, that she was adopted. In later years, she was inquisitive about her roots. Marga and I promised her that we would help her as soon as she was old enough. After graduating from high school, where she was voted as the most beautiful and the shyest, Inge attended an art college in Los Angeles to study graphic design.

Inge all grown up

Before my retirement in June of 1989 from General Motors after twenty-seven years of service, I was the sole photographer for the General Motors Plant One history book *From Gaslight to Starlight*.

The fascinating hobby of photography followed me through my whole life. Since I received many national and international awards, I became known in the media circles, and I decided to build our own business, a photographic studio. The adventure immediately became a success. Marga offered herself as my studio manager and was responsible for the sale, as well as customer care. She did an excellent job, and I was very proud of her sale performances.

Our indoor pool

With combined effort, we built our indoor swimming pool entirely ourselves and then used it as our photography studio. We even included a whirlpool and a sauna. Sometimes when I relaxed in our whirlpool, my memories went back to my little tin tub and the dreams of my childhood.

Our scenic bridge

In the forest terrain behind our house, I built a nature studio with a five-meter-high waterfall. A romantic bridge led the way over the scenic, beautiful creek.

The earnings of the photo studios was applied almost entirely to Inge's expensive education. Often, I called Los Angeles "the black hole" in which our profit was sucked in, but Marga and I were glad to grant Inge the best education we could.

Our Search for Inge's Origin

After Inge's graduation from the art collage, Marga and I decided to start our search for Inge's birth mother. We registered Inge with ALMA and attended some meetings. We wrote a letter to the honorable judge of the district court of Seattle with a plea to open the adoption records. There was no reply.

Finally, Marga and I decided to take matters in our own hands, and in September of 1992, we started our trip from Michigan to Los Angeles. Inge was able to take a few days off from her job to accompany us on our trip along the beautiful shoreline of California and Oregon to Seattle. It was one of the most memorable trips we have ever taken.

We arrived in Seattle on a Friday afternoon. The time was very short since Inge had to fly back to Los Angeles the coming Monday afternoon. We had only one hour to get to the courthouse to try to talk to the judge in person. At the information desk, we asked for the judge's room number. We were surprised when we entered a courtroom in the middle of a court session instead of an office.

As we stepped into the courtroom, the court secretary asked us to come to the bench, thinking we had something to do with the case. As Inge and I whispered to her the reason we were there, she told us that the records were closed permanently but referred us to the adoption record department. They, in turn, suggested trying a Washington state-based organization by the name of WARM (Washington Adoption Research Management). It was too late for that day, and we decided to find this organization early Monday morning since Inge had to fly back to L.A. that afternoon.

As we were sitting on that Friday evening at the restaurant on top of the Space Needle celebrating Marga's birthday, we had to admit there was not much hope of any success.

Monday morning after a long search, we found the office of WARM. They did not give us much hope but asked Inge to register for three hundred and fifty dollars. We decided not to register. As we left the office, it was about noon, and Inge's flight would leave at four. We knew from Inge's adoption papers and the day when we picked her up twenty-four years ago which hospital Inge was born at. Since we still had an hour to spare, I made the suggestion to find the hospital and ask for Inge's medical records. On our way, I said, "Maybe the record keeper does not know the rules and will give us more than just Inge's records."

At the hospital, the desk clerk dialed the number for records and handed Inge the phone. Inge asked the person on the other end for her medical records. When Inge laid the phone down, she said that she could pick the records up the next day and that the person was just a substitute for the regular record keeper, who was on vacation.

After we returned to the parking lot, I said to Inge, "Go back right now and ask the person if you could get the records today since you have to go back to L.A. and say that we also have to leave today. By tomorrow, the regular person in charge might be back from vacation."

While Marga and I waited in the car, Inge went back to the front desk. It seemed a long time before Inge came back, waving a brown envelope. Very excited, she stepped into the car. She said, "They gave me all the records. Hurry; let's leave before they realize that they made a mistake."

At the next curve, we studied the records with all the information about the birth mother, her husband, and the grandmother. Then we took Inge to the airport. Marga and I returned to the hotel and searched the Seattle phone directory, and from about three pages of people with the same last name, we found one match. However, it was a different address than the medical record showed. Would we still have the right person?

We called, but there was no answer, and we decided to try again later that day from a camping ground north of Seattle. When I called from there, a man answered the phone. I introduced myself briefly and asked if his wife gave birth to a little girl at the specific hospital in 1968. He stated, "We have been divorced for sixteen years, and yes, that's true, but I am not the father."

I answered, "Yes, I am aware of that." When I told him that I was the adoptive father and we were trying to find his ex-wife, he said, "This is the most beautiful message. My former wife's last name is now Smith, and we are still good friends. She has been searching for twelve years for the girl and will be very happy when I give her the news." Before I hung up, I told him that it would take us a week to get back to Michigan, and I asked him if he would tell his ex-wife to give us a call after our return.

I called Inge that night in L.A. and told her the good news. She was very excited.

We were back home in Michigan not more than an hour when we received a call from Inge's birth mother. She was so excited about the news and said that Inge had three siblings, two brothers and one sister, and that they were all very happy that we found them. We told her that we would call Inge first to bring her the good news and, after I talked to her, Inge would call her. The two talked that night for two hours.

A few days later we received a letter from Inge's birth mother explaining why she gave Inge up for adoption and that she was glad that Inge had a good home and a good upbringing. We, in turn, sent photographs from Inge and ourselves. We also sent a video I had edited from home movies for Inge's twenty-first birthday. The video consisted of scenes from her birth to the present. We thought that it was quite a treasure for her birth mother to see how the child she gave up grew up. Marga and I were so gratified finally meeting the woman who, through her sacrifice, gave us the greatest gift and so much happiness. Letters went back and forth, and on Thanksgiving Day, Inge went to Seattle to meet her birth mother and her siblings. It was a joyous three days for all of them.

The search for Inge's heritage was not complete without the finding of her birth father. Inge's birth mother did start a search for the man she knew twenty-four years ago and had not seen since. After a short search, she had found the address of two individuals with the same name, both of them in western Washington.

Later, when she found out that it was both the same person, she called him on the phone with the news that he had a daughter. Until that time, he was unaware of Inge's existence. Of course, he was shocked at first. He was still with the same woman as he was with twenty-four years ago, with whom he had three daughters, all about the same age as Inge. Since his wife had no idea about his affair, how would she react toward his confession? It took about three months until he told his wife and his daughters, and he then also finally contacted Inge.

In the summer of 1993, Marga and I went again to Seattle to meet with Inge, who came from L.A. to meet her additional family. From there, Inge, Marga, Inge's birth mother, and her husband started the trip to western Washington to accept the invitation to meet Inge's birth father and his wife.

When we finally arrived at the beautiful, romantic little valley, we found a very gentle man who could not deny being Inge's procreator. He had retired from the U.S. Air Force. It seemed a little strange that almost to the day, fifty years after an Allied bomb took the life of Marga's little sister Inge, we found the man who gave us Inge, our daughter, and he also served in the U.S. Air Force.

His wife was very charming, understanding, and kind. Sadly, we only met one of Inge's sisters while we were there. Her likeness with Inge was indisputable. The blissful reunion would not have taken place without the understanding and the support from Inge's new family extension.

We all are staying in close contact with each other. Inge's birth mother and her husband visited us in Michigan, and we had a few very nice days together. Inge went back to Los Angeles, working at a design company. Her assignments were the graphic designs to enhance the site of all nine stadiums hosting the World Cup of Soccer.

After a vacation in Florida in 1994, Marga and I decided to move to Florida. We ended our photographic business and sold our home in Michigan and moved in 1995.

Inge, with enormous achievement at her work, kept close contact with us. She met a great person and referred to him as her soul mate. His name is Kevin. He also studied graphic design and is very successful in his profession.

Inge and Kevin married in 1998 at an old church located in the beautiful region of the Dolomite Alps in northern Italy. With the birth of a boy named Leo Christopher in August of 2003, their life was whole.

When Inge and Kevin decided to move closer to us because we are not that young anymore, as Inge stated, they moved from California to Florida, and this made

Inge and Kevin's wedding, Dolomite Alps in Northern Italy

our life complete. Marga and I were blessed to see Leo grow from a baby to such a handsome little boy and have him and his wonderful parents so close by.

In 2001, Marga and I celebrated our golden wedding. The ceremony took place in my hometown of

Our Golden Wedding Anniversary, 2001

Remscheid in the same church we were married in fifty years ago.

We were very much surprised that some attendants were also present at our wedding ceremony fifty years ago.

The church we were married in, 1951.

Our marriage was quite a roller-coaster ride that went from cloud nine to broken hearts to cloud nine again, but our love for each other is immeasurable, and it never left us. We are the living proof that nothing can break a relationship if love is more than just a word. Sometimes I wonder how I would cope with the loss of my love if she would go before me.

By now, all my eight friends are gone, and from my ten siblings, only my ninety-one-year-old sister Gertrud, who is in a coma from a serious stroke, lives.

When one day I mentioned to my sister Gertrud that I had a good guardian angel, she replied, "One? There must be at least ten that protected you."

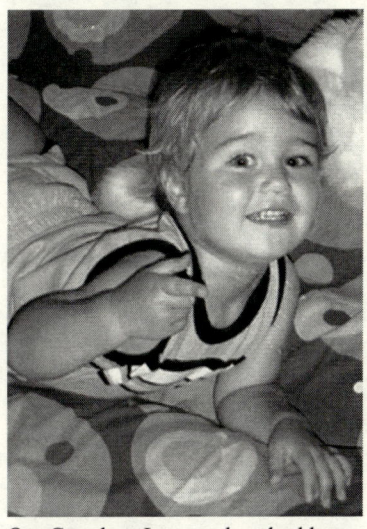

Our Grandson Leo, my best buddy.

I am concluding my life story, and for a while, it was a wild ride. Now that I am old, I have to thank my ten guardian angels for protecting me during my hard and dangerous life. If I could have one wish, I would like to ask them to protect my family: Inge, Kevin, and my little friend, my grandson, Leo, whom I love more than myself. Please give them the protection you have given me during my whole life.

And for you, Leo, I hope you learned from my mistakes and also from a few good deeds. When you are old enough to read all this, I will most likely not be with you on this earth any longer, but we will meet again at a more peaceful place someday. I am so appreciative that I was able to experience the unconditional love you gave me. Do not forget what you have promised me. If your wish to be an astronaut becomes someday a reality, look through the window of your spaceship to search for me. You will definitely find me.